YOUR

MONEY

NARRATIVE

What's your story?

Amy R Cook

AMY R. COOK, CFP®

YOUR
MONEY
NARRATIVE

Understanding Your Story
to Build a Stronger
Financial Future

Advantage | Books

Published by Advantage Books, Charleston, South Carolina.
An imprint of Advantage Media.

ADVANTAGE is a registered trademark, and the Advantage colophon is a trademark of Advantage Media Group, Inc.

Printed in the United States of America.

10 9 8 7 6 5 4 3 2 1

ISBN: 978-1-64225-624-6 (Hardcover)
ISBN: 978-1-64225-623-9 (eBook)

Library of Congress Control Number: 2023911205

Book design by Wesley Strickland.

This publication is designed to provide accurate and authoritative information in regard to the subject matter covered. It is sold with the understanding that the publisher is not engaged in rendering legal, accounting, or other professional services. If legal advice or other expert assistance is required, the services of a competent professional person should be sought.

The opinions voiced in this material are for general information only and are not intended to provide specific advice or recommendations for any individual. All investing involves risk, including loss of principal. No strategy assures success or protects against loss.

Advantage Books is an imprint of Advantage Media Group. Advantage Media helps busy entrepreneurs, CEOs, and leaders write and publish a book to grow their business and become the authority in their field. Advantage authors comprise an exclusive community of industry professionals, idea-makers, and thought leaders. For more information go to **advantagemedia.com**.

To my dad,

Thank you for your endless support and enthusiasm around all my ideas, entrepreneurial spirit, optimism, and always making me laugh despite the circumstance. The values and principles you instilled are in my heart and head in all that I do. I wish you could have read this book; I miss you every day but know I will see you again someday.

JOHN F. MARTIN
1938–2007

CONTENTS

LET ME TELL YOU A STORY

W E HUMANS HAVE COMMUNICATED THROUGH
storytelling for thousands of generations. Well
before the invention of writing, it was the
stories told around the evening fire that passed wisdom from
family to family, generation to generation. Our elders, who
had amassed a lifetime of stories, were revered.

However, in our current world of bite-sized electronic
factoids and company pronouncements from on high, stories
and the art of storytelling have been pushed aside. Companies
tell us about their wonderful products and services. They communicate in dry corporatespeak. They sell, sell, and sell again.

Think about the difference between a typical company
brochure and a beautiful short story. One is sterile, facts

created by faceless marketers to persuade potential customers. The other is full of emotion and meaning. As you read a story, you're right there inside the unique circumstances, cheering for the characters.

We love stories!

Imagine you're at a cocktail party. If someone says, "Let me tell you a story about how I went from being poor to becoming rich," you're interested, right?

However, if someone were to say, "Let me tell you about the importance of investing," is your reaction the same?

The first story about money I remember hearing was at my high school investment club. The teacher who served as our advisor shared with us a little of his own money narrative. He said that public school teachers like him don't make much money, but anybody who spends less than what they make and invests wisely can build wealth. It was this single line that I remember to this day, forty years later: "Nobody gets rich on a salary."

The world doesn't need another traditional book about investing and other aspects of managing money. Heck, the personal finance category on Amazon lists some one thousand books on the subject. However, what's lacking in these titles is an understanding of personal finance based on how people think of money in the real world. What's lacking are stories.

Your Money Narrative is a different kind of personal finance book. It deftly shows us the many ways that people use and abuse money. Rather than preaching about the dos and don'ts of the financial world, we learn through the interesting stories of young and old, rich and poor, people who are smart with money and those who aren't.

Amy R. Cook is the ideal person to write *Your Money Narrative*. As you'll read in the opening chapter, her own money narrative shaped who she became, a top financial planning professional who runs her own business advising clients about their money narratives.

The stories you will read in these pages will help you to understand the fundamentals in an approachable and memorable way. Reading Amy's words, I imagined listening to her telling these stories to a rapt audience around a firepit. And just like stories told throughout time, instead of a collection of facts we forget, reading *Your Money Narrative* delivers wisdom about money we can use throughout our lives.

I never forgot that first memorable story about money that I heard as a teenager. And I used that wisdom, living my life based on what I learned from that story. As a result, I've enjoyed a life of wealth and happiness.

May your money narrative be equally positive.

DAVID MEERMAN SCOTT

Business growth strategist and *Wall Street Journal* bestselling author of thirteen books, including *Fanocracy*

1

WE ALL HAVE A MONEY NARRATIVE

WHEN I WAS FIVE, MY DAD TAUGHT ME HOW TO ride a bicycle. The very next day, we headed to the desert, and he taught me how to ride my first motorcycle, a Yamaha YZ50. I remember how excited he was to teach me how to ride my new minibike. My dad assured me that if I could ride a bike, I could ride a motorcycle. He had a lot of confidence in my ability considering I had just learned to ride a bike the day before; I was scared. I'll never forget the sound of the motor gurgling and how the handlebars vibrated beneath my tiny palms when I first settled on the seat. My dad gripped the back as he walked alongside me, demonstrating how to twist the throttle. Too much of a pull jerked me forward and too little kept me unmoving, so it took some time to find the perfect hand motion. When I eventually got it right, my speeding heart rate settled down, and my palms dried up, giving way to a new feeling—elation. At first, I was only allowed to stay close and follow the mini "track" he built for me, which was basically a big circle. As my fear subsided, my speed increased, and by the end of the weekend, I whipped along the trails, smiling through the cloud of sand that kicked up from my spinning tires. Well, that's how I remember it now, anyway.

I was inflated with confidence. At the time, I thought I was simply happy that I had a new way of getting around and I could try to keep up with my brothers. Looking back, I realized that it's more about the *feeling* that came with this new skill that truly marked this moment, embedding it in my memory.

On many weekends, I'd gear up and get to go to the desert or the races with my dad and brothers. As I stood on the sidelines time and time again, I asked my dad if I could race too. The answer was a hard no, which he said was my mom's decision. The reason was simply that it was too dangerous ... for a girl. At the time, I felt it was unfortunate to be a girl.

That was when my persistence started to shine. I made it my mission to beg and plead with her to let me race, making all kinds of promises and promoting myself as capable of "keeping up with the boys."

It never worked, and it became a recurring theme in my childhood. Not only could my brothers do more because they were older and bigger, but they were allowed more freedom in general because they were boys. I understand now that this protection was out of love and concern, but it never stopped me from fighting the perceived injustice and trying to win where I could and prove myself. As it turned out, being the little sister and the baby of the family proved to have its advantages, especially with my dad.

My relentless efforts continued, and they finally agreed to let me enter a "bicycle" race. I was very excited and nervous to show what I could do on the big day. It was a race of two, me and one other little girl; the result was devastating. As much as I wanted to win, I fell short and was lapped by my competition. I broke down in tears and cried. Initially, my dad tried to rationalize the situation and said I came in second place, which came with a trophy. But, even at five, I knew that second place in a race of two only meant one thing: there was one winner and one loser, and I lost. My dad put his hand on my shoulder and convincingly told me that I had lost because she had a far lighter and "better" bike than I did and that he couldn't afford to buy me a bike like that.

Aah … okay. If we had more money, I'd have won the race. This experience formed my first money narrative. The future would prove that although I have a competitive spirit, athleticism was not my strong suit, and it probably had nothing to do with the bike at all, but nonetheless, it was comforting at the time.

A couple of years later, my parents hit hard financial times, and our house, which sat at the top of the hill, up a long, windy driveway in the canyon, went into foreclosure, and we had to move. As I watched my dad's incredible stress, I decided that money was again the missing component. Another money narrative was formed. At seven, I had no context around the situation and formed an opinion and decision based on the facts as I saw them.

My dad spoke transparently about our financial position daily, so there were no surprises. We all knew our situation. He was gifted with finding humor in all situations, and this was no exception. There was a constant ebb and flow of being broke and having enough to get by. But when it came to certain occasions, the money seemed to appear miraculously. Christmas was always magical, filled with things we never imagined receiving during the rest of the year.

$ $ $

My dad's stress surrounding finances didn't go unnoticed by me. Even at a young age, I remember a constant undertone of urgency regarding money. It was like the background music on my childhood playlist, just loud enough to hear over the eighties and nineties soundtracks that rippled through our home. During these years, the weekly pizza day at school or the occasional skate night was not guaranteed; our situation seemed to change from week to week. But somehow, Christmas never missed us, and once a year, the gifts under the Christmas tree shined with newness. Back then, it was a miracle; today I imagine it created additional stress to figure out how to make that happen.

The constant rumblings about money in my home shaped my little brain into believing that more money was the solution to all of life's problems. In some ways, this was true. With more money, we could pay the mortgage and hold onto my parent's American dream that they were so proud of. With more money, I would've had a better bike, and I would've been the girl winning the race. Maybe more money would have relieved my dad's stress and the heart issues soon to surface. If you grow up with enough money, then it becomes less of an issue—almost nonexistent. But when you grow up in a family where conversations around money and the hope of having more are the average dinner conversation, well, money becomes everything. Money would have solved some of these problems, no doubt, but the question that never occurred to me was, "How much *more* did we need?" Would $1,000 solve our problems? $10,000? $100,000? $1,000,000? More importantly, was this about money at all?

My money narrative was clear: I had fear around money and not having enough. The glaring problem was that I was clinging to a story without all the facts and details. Without all the details, it can feel like an uphill battle trying to find a solution.

These early determinations served me in some ways; I ventured out to make a few bucks on my own, starting at around eleven with a paper route, followed by many more jobs throughout my teen years. My parents always supported my initiatives, from lemonade stands to forming my own "babysitters' club," and even made me business cards to hand out. For me, the idea of being able to do something that generated money was directly attached to a sense of security. The problem was that from one venture and dollar to the next, fear continued to grip me. I hadn't determined how much was needed or what I was trying to accomplish, so I continued to stack my dollars with no idea about how big the stack should be, which naturally resulted in disappointment.

Unsurprisingly, most people immediately think of money when they hear the word "security." We are bombarded with terms like "financial security," "securing your financial future," and a thousand other terms relating to money management. Even the portion of the US federal government that administers retirement, disability, and survivor benefits has the word in it. Social *Security*. For most people, financial security equates to peace of mind.

As a child, I learned quickly that more money would solve all our problems and remove the threat of losing safety and protection. Fear can have a powerful grip and snowball into more catastrophic fears that aren't based on reality. I feared living under a bridge with a shopping cart in tow, even though my real life never got to a place that was anywhere near that. In actuality, even during difficult financial times, my parents always looked after us and provided for us.

The bridge entered my thoughts again when I found myself divorced at twenty-five, single-handedly responsible for two young children with only a high school degree and minimal job experience.

I was frightened, with a million thoughts running through my mind and past money fears resurfacing like an old enemy that had grown significantly in size. I was no longer responsible for just myself, but also had two little girls to care for. My determination was bolstered to fight the statistics I knew I was facing, and true to my early money narrative, I only saw two options: sink or swim. I knew I had to swim. As a single mom with no skill set to put me at an advantage, I took on multiple jobs to get the ball (and cash flow) rolling. It wasn't adding up.

More than anything, I wanted to keep my house and the security it provided. After working a bunch of part-time jobs, I got a job doing administrative work for an architectural firm. When the in-house notary left the company, I eagerly offered to obtain the licensing to fill the gap. I utilized this additional credential to pick up extra work at night doing mortgage loan signings, which turned into a steady contract with multiple jobs coming in each week. It didn't take me long to realize that my evening loan-signing gigs were adding up to nearly as much as my day job in less time.

As I went through stacks of documents in the evenings, my comfort and familiarity increased. I knew I needed a path to increase my income potential, and at the time a real estate license was all that was needed to go into the mortgage business. With my dad's entrepreneurial optimism and encouragement to go for it, I got licensed, created a reserve cushion with a loan on the house (in hindsight, a risky decision that could have been a disaster), and jumped in with all that I had, determined to succeed. With it being the early 2000s and interest rates moving to all-time lows, timing was on my side. I was on the phone nonstop, and application packages poured in. Within a couple of months, I was at the top of the list of around forty loan originators in our office month after month. I became a success story despite the odds stacked against me. When people would ask what my secret was or how I was doing so well in the business, I didn't know the answer. It didn't feel like I was doing anything special other than talking with people all day and helping them with possible solutions; my peers were doing the same thing. In hindsight, it was bigger than that; as I worked to diffuse my fears around money, I became attentive and empathic in helping others try to do the same.

Through the years, I have learned to cut myself some slack; perfection is impossible, and growth comes from life's ups and downs and decisions we make along the way. The allure of financial planning is that it is both proactive and progressive; we all can be active players in our own stories. Sure, there are things we can't control in life, but we can all choose to take control of our household financial decisions. Planning with intention and purpose feels really good too.

When I transitioned into the financial planning industry, I continued to learn and fill my education gaps. I worked full time while pursuing a bachelor's degree, followed by the Certified Financial Planner certification and a master's degree in personal financial planning. The studies about behavioral finance opened my eyes to many of my own money narratives and eventually resulted in this book.

My money narrative has dramatically changed over the years, and yours can too. By clearly defining my goals, I was able to slowly move the needle and remove emotion with daily financial decisions. Like any other skill, it takes practice … and more practice. As Lewis Carroll famously said, "If you don't know where you're going, any road will take you there."[1]

Financial goals are like other goals that we set out to achieve. When one goal is reached, we may set a new one or make a change midway. If there is a setback, adjustments may be necessary. Consistency is key to growth, and by tackling different things in stages, successful outcomes emerge over time and habits are formed.

It is not a coincidence that my path led to a career as a financial planner. As I worked toward eliminating my own fear around money, I helped others do the same. I feel grateful and blessed to be a part of my clients' lives and financial team as a source of guidance, encouragement, and friendship as they craft their own unique financial blueprint and legacy.

Your Money Narrative

My money narrative will be different from yours simply because we all have unique stories and have experienced life differently.

---

1   Lewis Carroll, *Alice's Adventures in Wonderland*, Oxford, 1865.

The money narrative of a sixty-something newly retired couple will be very different from that of a twenty-something single person starting out in a professional job. The same is true for that of someone who is married without children versus someone who is married with several children.

As David said in his foreword, we humans are natural storytellers. Long before the written word, we were telling stories to communicate with others and to process information in our own minds. Stories are the heart of human existence, and whether you realize it or not, a scene is always unfolding itself in the inner workings of your brain. Money stories are no different. When you become aware of your own money narratives, you can question their validity, think about how they came to be, and modify them if they are not beneficial as you work toward your goals.

Money narratives can be passed down within families and cultures and are often partial truths based on our unique experiences or from others who passed them down to us. We each hold our own version of the "truth," but the defining question to consider is whether these beliefs are helping us achieve our goals or undermining our progress.

For example, the Great Depression formed money narratives based on deprivation and poverty. Young adults coming out of this era were afraid to spend money and held on to things for fear they wouldn't be able to replace them. As financial means increased, the habits and internal beliefs didn't just disappear; they were carried on for decades and passed on to future generations.

Long before money was invented, people bartered for goods and services as a means of survival. The ability to trade items was a gateway that allowed people to obtain items they wanted and needed. But, in its most basic form, money is paper. Our decisions around money are not about the sheets of green printed paper we exchange or the numbers we see on a bank or investment statement; they are about survival, taking care of the people we love, giving back, and leaving a legacy that is meaningful.

This book is a culmination of short stories based on fictional characters with relatable dilemmas you may identify with—either in your life or with someone you know. You may discover money narratives that changed your life in a positive way or uncover stories that need an update. Either way, by pulling the curtain back and examining your own money narratives, you can determine if they are aligned with your financial goals and the legacy you want to leave behind.

There are questions at the end of each chapter and checklists that can be accessed through the *Your Money Narrative* website at www.YourMoneyNarrative.com or via the QR code. The purpose of the questions is to inspire thoughts and ideas. The checklists, on the other hand, can serve as road maps for different financial stages and significant financial decisions you may be experiencing now or down the line. Ideally, the questions and checklists will initiate discussions among you, your loved ones, and, above all, yourself.

2

THE REAL ESTATE PACT

C HINESE FOOD HAD BEEN THE GO-TO CHOICE for the Smith and Wells families on New Year's Eve. Since they started celebrating the holiday together several years ago, it had always been an assortment of appetizers from their favorite local Chinese restaurant, but this year would be different. They would have to select a new restaurant to satisfy their holiday appetites.

"I can't decide." Sophia, overwhelmed at the options on the menu, pushed the folded piece of paper across the table in the vacation home the two families had decided to rent for a getaway. Tucked away at the end of a narrow road, a three-hour drive from their year-round homes, the beach house was a perfect way to celebrate their family friendship.

"You've always been so picky about trying out new places." Clara received the takeout menu, glanced at it once, and decided for the four adults and four children that they would be having a double order of every appetizer, minus the spare ribs, a slight diversion from past New Year's Eves.

"Maybe you're too easy to please," Sophia retorted with a laugh, knowing that her best friend of thirty-five years would find the humor.

"You two sound like an old married couple," said Ben, Sophia's husband, not taking his eyes off the Lego castle he was building with the two boys on the floor.

Two boys and two girls. It was exactly how Sophia and Clara planned their futures when they were little girls, joined at the hip through all of life's ups and downs. They had always hoped the men they chose to marry would get along like best friends too, and that is exactly where they landed. Tonight, on the eve of 1985, their two families were celebrating the holiday away, in a home they took great care in choosing.

Now, as the women sat across from one another plucking the ingredients of Chex Mix from a bowl between them, they chatted about how nice the house was.

"How amazing would it be to own a house like this?" Sophia said as she ran a palm over the dips and bumps of the worn picnic table that had been repurposed as one of the two dinner tables in the home. A table for kids and a table for adults, just like when they shared Thanksgivings together in their homes.

Ben perked up at the idea, pulling himself upright on the floor after he locked a Lego in place. "So let's do it."

"What are we doing?" Clara's husband, Jim, paused the sporting event that was playing on the television, freezing two players in place on the screen.

"Let's buy a house together!" Ben shot up to a standing position. "I mean, think about it, we celebrate every holiday together, and we've never had a disagreement."

Sophia shot a raised eyebrow at Clara, who retorted with a smirk. "We fight all the time. You were just saying we bicker like an old married couple."

Ben pushed his hands out in front of him, palms up. "I mean a real fight. Something that doesn't involve the selection of appetizers." Ben began to pace the room, spinning into another idea. "And think about how much we'd save. We could each pay 50 percent of the down payment, split the mortgage, and share the house."

He paused, dissecting a few thoughts that came to mind.

"And if we ever need solo family time, well, we agree on certain weekends being for one family and other weekends being for the other family."

"Do you honestly think these two are going to have solo time? It will be more likely they'll have the place to themselves for a week away from us," Jim added.

"True," Sophia and Clara responded at the same time, nodding in agreement, the idea shaping itself in their minds and quickly becoming a potential reality. It was similar to when they sealed the deal with their parents the first time they had a sleepover.

"Imagine what it will be like when our kids are grown up and they have their own children." Clara brought up the future, a conversation they had been having since before they even had children. "We could hand the house down to them and leave a legacy behind."

"I did just inherit that money." Sophia threw the statement into the space between the four of them.

"And we have that chunk of savings we still have no idea what to do with." Clara turned to Jim.

"What could be wrong with it? It's a win-win for all of us." Ben waved his hand in the direction of the boys on the floor, still lost in their Lego world, and then at the two girls doing a puzzle at a nearby table.

What Are the Smith and Wells Families' Money Narratives?

Clearly, these two couples have a wonderful relationship and a great deal of trust within their circle. From the planning lens, sometimes I feel like I am the downer at the party when looking at various pros and cons of decisions. Ultimately, the goal is to mitigate as much risk as possible for a greater likelihood of success.

There are two types of risk—perceived and actual. Perceived risk, on a basic level, is subjective to each person and can vary greatly based on individual emotions and past experiences that we carry through life. Have you ever seen someone so worried about something that seems so unlikely to you but very real to the other person? That is perceived risk, and oftentimes, while something is statistically very unlikely, it can take control of us and feel incredibly real.

Actual risk is quantifiable; there is data to back it up. Your automobile insurance premium is based on many factors, including your age, gender, history, and even your occupation. Actuarial specialists can establish "odds" of accidents and claims based on these factors. This is why teenagers typically have the highest premiums.

When I was in my early twenties, I agreed to finance a car for someone close to me. At the time, I believed this person would make the payments as promised. This story could have resulted in many different outcomes and could easily have gone as planned, but it didn't. The vehicle ended up in an accident and was deemed unsalvageable by the insurance company. It didn't take long for me to learn that the person I set out to help had stopped making the car payments. What started as an arrangement between friends quickly turned into a nightmare.

I didn't understand the risks involved in the title being in my name and the responsibility that went along with what happened to the car whether or not I was driving it. However, I quickly learned that the insurance companies and the bank had little concern for who was driving the car, and instead they were more focused on who was *responsible* for it.

Unfortunately, the amount of money the insurance company was willing to pay was far less than what was owed to the bank, resulting in a deficit that I spent years paying off. There was adequate insurance in place to compensate the other driver and their vehicle expenses because, otherwise, the situation could have been far worse. The person who I helped disappeared, and I was left holding the bag. It was a difficult and costly lesson but valuable in understanding *actual* risk in financial decisions. On the other hand, if I allowed this experience to permanently alter my ability to trust the intentions of others, it would be *perceived* risk. Fortunately, this did not happen.

> There are two types of risk—perceived and actual.

This early financial mistake was not lost on me, and the experience embedded an awareness inside me that has helped me and many others over the years when analyzing risk relating to financial planning decisions.

The Smiths and Wells will be required to have homeowner's insurance on their new beach cottage; they will each have to qualify individually for their portion of the mortgage. This all looks great, so what can go wrong?

The worst thing that could happen in this situation is for life to go in an unexpected direction and throw a wrench in their tight-knit/close relationship. The best way to avoid this is to have candid and thorough conversations before they sign the paperwork and ensure they are on the same page with the decision to purchase the home together and overall expectations.

The two couples should discuss the impact of purchasing the home for both of them. Is it an uncomfortable stretch financially for either couple? Do they both have adequate reserves in addition to the down payment? As a rule of thumb, each couple should have a minimum of three months of living expenses for their households and three months' worth of their portion of the new second home expenses. We want to make sure that if one of them loses their job, they can maintain their portion of the expenses while they look for a new job.

What happens if one couple wants to sell the property at some point? A written legal agreement could include these "what if" scenarios/clauses and how each would be handled.

If one person passes away, is the widow/widower individually able to maintain their half of the transaction? If not, one possible solution is life insurance and a buy/sell agreement. This would allow the insurance contracts to step in and pay a death benefit that could be used to pay off the affected couple's portion of the mortgage.

With any joint purchase or investment involving a loan, debt obligation, and an ongoing financial commitment, there are many considerations to ensure proper planning and protection for all parties involved. In this situation, I would start with some ground rules followed with "what if" and "should we" questions. As I shared in my story about the car loan, costly consequences could have been avoided had I gone through a risk analysis prior to making a decision.

Does each spouse have equal voting rights, or will they predetermine a course of action for various circumstances? How will the property be titled? Will they create a separate entity, such as a limited liability company (LLC), for tax purposes? What if one couple wants to sell and the other does not? Is there a predetermined buyout clause? What if one couple decides to divorce? How will it be handled if one couple cannot pay the mortgage? Should we establish a dedicated account with reserves? Is the option open to rent the property if they are not using it as much as anticipated? What parameters will they use to gauge this? How do they want the property to be passed on to the next generation? If one couple passes away, will there be a buyout agreement, or will the children inherit their portion of the house for continued use?

Although the property will be a combined family property with years of priceless memories, it is also a financial commitment. Properly establishing this agreement will mitigate risk and protect both families and their children. There is a lot to think about, and without a crystal ball, no one knows which scenarios will come up in the future. However, conversations about these things in the present will prove valuable when/ if they do.

I would recommend meeting with a real estate attorney to explore the various structures available and what would make the most sense for their situation.

By addressing and adding protection around actual risks with the transaction, they will have peace of mind and can move forward with this exciting new stage of life. Otherwise, perceived risk can creep into the picture over time and create unnecessary concerns and worries.

Questions to Consider

- ➔ Are you planning a large purchase or investment in the next five years?
- ➔ If so, have you thought through some of the legal and financial aspects in the story?
- ➔ Are there gaps that you are unclear on that need more research?

Do

- ➔ Discuss and create a plan for large purchases (house or rental property) before you start the process.
- ➔ Do your due diligence on professionals hired and the overall process, including additional unexpected expenses.
- ➔ Ensure you are adequately prepared financially. If not, put a plan in place with a timeline to achieve the goal.

Don't

- ➔ Jump into a large purchase/commitment without knowing all the details and ensuring you are ready.
- ➔ Try to do it all yourself; a professional team can be invaluable.
- ➔ Avoid it altogether if it seems overwhelming.

Real estate/home ownership can be a valuable component of your overall investment portfolio. A fixed-rate mortgage provides a consistent payment with the debt decreasing over time, which you will eventually pay off. There are also tax benefits associated with home ownership. If you are conflicted about whether you are ready to purchase a home, it may be beneficial to consult a financial professional for assistance with a rent-versus-own analysis. If purchasing a home is not feasible at the moment, you can develop a plan to gradually save for a down payment to prepare for the future.

3

THE TEENAGE ENTREPRENEUR

WITH BOTH PARENTS WORKING FROM HOME, Megan was always greeted by her mom or dad when she got off the school bus that delivered her to the nearby stop. Today, neither parent had afternoon meetings, and they were both available to accompany their daughter as she stepped off the middle school bus. Like always, she filled them in on her day, including all the antics of the teen drama that ricocheted off the walls of her seventh-grade classroom.

And then, out of nowhere, following a rant about how the lunchroom options were too limited for her, she started in on her career aspirations.

"I think it's time I get a job." Megan dropped the words into the conversation as they trudged up the hill to their home.

It wasn't the first time the girl had thought about making her own money. From a very young age, Megan developed a natural interest in the growth of money. She got it honestly, as both her parents had always conveyed the fun aspects of making money. Seldom did her mother and father complain about their jobs. Instead, they expressed their entrepreneurial spirit and made sure to celebrate the big wins they had with each of their businesses. One of these occasions was when they set aside a weekly amount for a trip to Disney World when Megan was nine years old. Unlike many families, Megan was part of the entire planning process, continuously keeping tabs on how their vacation account was growing and even contributing her birthday money to put them over the edge of the goal. It was as if the family was participating in a race together, and they cheered one another on as they crossed the finish line.

Having witnessed the thrill of achieving a financial goal firsthand, it was no surprise that Megan wanted to start earning her own money, and she made it clear to her parents what her goals were.

"I want to save enough money for a new iPad," Megan said.

By the time they arrived at their front door, Megan had laid out the plans for how much she would need to save to purchase the technology. At the kitchen table, she took it a step further and created a bullet point list of the potential jobs she could work at her age. Much to her chagrin, thirteen-year-olds couldn't legally work in her state, but she had her own ideas about how she could make some cash without having to sign an I-9 form.

As she pointed to the sheet, she presented her options to her parents, who were listening to their daughter with a glimmer of pride in their eyes.

"I could rake leaves." Megan extended an arm in the direction of the expansive window that looked out into their own yard, which was a blurry layer of red, yellow, and orange leaves.

"Can you start with our yard?" her dad joked.

Megan kept to her task at hand and pushed past her father's humor. "I know for certain that Miss Adams across the street will hire me. The Smith boys were supposed to rake for her, and they didn't show up, so I'm a shoo-in."

Both her parents stood in front of her and nodded as she continued.

"I'm already certified from that babysitter course, so I could update my CPR certification with the rest of my birthday money and then start advertising for babysitting jobs. We all know there is a dire need for this in our neighborhood alone," Megan said matter-of-factly, referring to the plethora of homes with children under nine in their neighborhood.

"I like how you're considering how you will pay for the necessities of your job." Her mother smiled.

"And finally, I think it's time I open my own bank account." She said the words confidently as she envisioned checking the final item off of her list.

If her parents were surprised by her go-getter attitude, they didn't show it. Instead, they both nodded their heads in agreement. As entrepreneurs themselves, they made it very clear they were Megan's biggest fans, and they were thrilled that she was displaying the drive to achieve goals on her own at such a young age. At the age of eleven, she pulled weeds from the crevices of their garden, making one dollar a bag. At twelve, she spent two hours after school several days a week working for five dollars an hour as a mother's helper. She was more than capable of babysitting and raking leaves at thirteen years old.

What's Megan's Money Narrative?

Megan is off to a great start; she has the motivation and drive to accomplish her goals. The first goal is an iPad; however, it can lead to much bigger goals when she gains momentum. It is great to see her parents involving her in the saving process, and because of that, she witnessed firsthand that the Disney World money didn't just appear. It took commitment, dedication, and time to reach that goal. It was also a great opportunity for her

> Money doesn't just appear; it takes commitment, dedication, and time to reach your financial goals.

parents to insert teaching lessons as the money was accumulating, which will naturally build solid financial habits that will likely stay with her through life.

I remember the excitement of earning money at a young age and being able to buy things with my own money. It's all surplus when expenses are zero or close to it. It always felt good to have some money in the bank, and true to my early money narratives, I made sure that I always did.

This probably doesn't come as a big surprise, but my favorite class in high school was economics. One of the class projects involved choosing individual stock positions and monitoring them over time. Back then, we couldn't check this online because that didn't exist yet. We had to look at the newspaper daily and check the prices and movement of the stock positions.

My dad knew the drill and started setting aside the business section for me, and we would look at it together when he got home from work. He embraced my enthusiasm and offered to help me actually buy shares of stock, so the homework felt as if it was like a real job. He said that he would match what I bought; so if I bought one share, he bought one too. My little brain quickly calculated the win in the situation, and I was all in. Essentially, it was like a 401(k) match at a company—free money.

I was babysitting a lot; I had regular jobs almost every day and preferred to spend my weekends babysitting and rarely turned down a job. I wanted to put everything I made into purchasing more shares.

My dad didn't anticipate the investment level to be so high, and he had to put a cap on the matched funds similar to what employers do with a company 401(k). The match he provided gave me an immediate win, and I also learned about compounding (reinvesting stock-paid dividends into more shares) and dollar cost averaging (systematic purchases of shares regardless of the price).

Every day, I watched as the shares went up and down, and it wasn't long before I grew comfortable with the process. Eventually, I sold them; it would be later in life that I began to *buy and hold* over long periods of time.

My early investing story is a great memory, and my dad's willingness to invest a couple hundred bucks to bring my school project to life was a gift that continues to pay dividends.

> My dad's willingness to invest a couple hundred bucks to bring my school project to life was a gift that continues to pay dividends.

As far as Megan is concerned, her parents could consider helping her establish an investment account (in addition to the bank account). By doing this, she would be able to make small monthly deposits as she works toward her other goal of purchasing the iPad.

If Megan takes 20 percent off the top of what she earns and invests it, she will be creating a lifelong habit of paying herself first. Kids have a great opportunity in this regard because they are not yet strapped with adult life responsibilities and bills. If she maintains the habit of investing a percentage of everything she makes, she will be happy she did later. It may seem like a small amount of money, but it can turn into larger amounts over time. This account could be used to purchase a car or something more significant, such as a down payment on a home, if she consistently cultivates this habit and commitment.

When Megan is a little older and gets a regular hourly job, she should consider opening a Roth IRA. She can contribute to a Roth as long as she has earned income; the money she contributes to this account will grow tax-free for her eventual retirement. Current guidelines also allow for a one-time penalty-free redemption from a Roth IRA for a first-time homebuyer as long as she has the Roth for at least five years, so a portion of this account could be used for that if she chooses.

If Megan's parents are able to do so, they could match some of her contributions in the new account, setting their daughter up for long-term success. Megan is in an optimal position to start on the right foot for financial success.

Questions to Consider

➜ Are you having basic financial/money management conversations with your kids?

➜ Are you including them in parts of the household finances where they are involved, such as vacations, college planning, etc.?

➜ Have you asked your financial advisor to talk with your teen/preteen about financial planning basics when they show interest?

Do

➔ Talk to your kids about money and involve them in financial decision-making in areas that involve them (a family night out or saving up for something).

➔ Consider playing age-appropriate board games that involve careers and money and correlate it to real life or people they know.

➔ Encourage them to establish their own bank/savings account and list goals, and monitor them together.

Don't

➔ Assume they are learning about money management in school.

➔ Avoid financial conversations to protect them. The more kids learn about money at home, the better start they will have as young adults when they are thrown into "adulting."

Whether you enjoy discussing financial topics or avoid them as much as possible, money plays a part in our lives. It is essential in our world and allows us to do things we want to do and support ourselves and those we love. If we spend all our money, we end up broke. If we save all our money, we might miss out on things we enjoy doing. If we take the emotion out of money/financial topics and put a plan in place that directs our money where to go, we can help our kids set up similar habits so that they can do the same.

4

JUST GETTING STARTED

OLIVER AND EMMA WERE STILL ON CLOUD NINE from having their first baby. The couple had been married and living together for five years, and they were more than excited to add to their family, already checking off items on their new parenting to-do list. While at Emma's cousin Abby's house for a weekly family dinner, a conversation about "adulting" came up. Having spent the last few years slipping into the role of real adulthood where they were paying bills and now taking care of a small human, Oliver and Emma could relate. They both laughed as they shared their opinion on the topic.

"Gosh, it seems like just yesterday we were sleeping in late and catching up on our favorite sitcoms on the weekends," Emma said as she passed baby Eleanor to Abby's open arms.

"What weekends?" Oliver chuckled.

"Now it seems like every spare moment is spent paying bills or trying to figure out how to pay bills."

"I can relate," Abby added. "Seems like just yesterday I had one of these little babies in my arms, and now my babies are nearly as tall as me." She adjusted the bib on Eleanor as she continued. "Have you guys thought about ways you can cut down on bills so you can focus on that home down payment you're striving for in three years?"

The weekly dinners often led to them discussing goals that they shared with Emma's cousin, and she was well aware that they were saving to buy a home.

A wave of guilt passed over Emma's face. "We're still trying to decide which daycare Eleanor should attend after my maternity leave is over. We're still registered for two places but can't decide."

Abby came back with several questions involving their monthly bills, ones that neither one of them had given much thought to. They had gotten used to paying bills, but they didn't know there were possibilities for minimizing payments depending on the monthly plans they were on.

"Write them down." Abby pulled a piece of paper out of a nearby drawer. "Write all your bills down and how much you pay."

"Okay," Oliver said, always up for a challenge.

Much to their surprise, they were overpaying for not one but several of their monthly expenses. One of those expenses was a $200 cable bill with premium movie channels that they never watched.

"When was the last time we actually watched live TV?" Emma inquired as she twisted her neck toward Oliver.

"Um, before Eleanor was born."

"I think we can survive on cutting the cable and just using Netflix and a couple of other streaming services," Emma said.

Another item that Abby brought to their attention was their cell phone plans. "I remember how much we saved when we consolidated our plan. It's quite shocking," Abby said, as she swayed side to side with a now-sleeping Eleanor.

Now excited about the dollar signs she was seeing, Emma threw another suggestion into the conversation. "What about our cars?"

"What about them?" Oliver raised his brows as he looked up from typing notes on his phone, a list of to-dos for their new money-saving goals.

"Well, we both work from home at least 50 percent of the time. And we never have to be in different places at the same time. So, why don't we get rid of one vehicle?"

"Now we're talking!" Abby gently dropped into the chair, keeping her eyes locked on Eleanor.

Dollar signs shot through Emma's and Oliver's minds as they continued to brainstorm money-saving ideas. They needed all the extra cash they could get with both of them working modest jobs and the added funds involved with a new baby. One of the things that they had going for them was that they'd both tackled and paid off their student loans before starting a family.

What's Oliver and Emma's Money Narrative?

First, congratulations to Oliver and Emma for taking this step at a young age. I often wonder why basic financial planning is not taught in high school as a standard course to better prepare kids for an inevitable part of life—managing their money. Regardless of our material aspirations, we all have to manage our expenses and take care of ourselves as adults.

> Regardless of our material aspirations, we all have to manage our expenses and take care of ourselves as adults.

Oliver and Emma are ahead of their peers in getting help with this at a young age, which is great. The first step is to figure out where they are now. They can start with a financial report card that showcases what they are doing optimally and what needs work, so they know where they stand and where the current gaps can be minimized.

Starting with a budget worksheet is great, but we need to make sure the numbers are accurate. I recommend filling out the worksheet and comparing it against bank statements to ensure the numbers line up by downloading the last six months and establishing averages for things like groceries and utility bills.

I would advise Oliver and Emma to pay off any outstanding credit card debt before considering investing; they'll free up additional cash flow to invest in other things by eliminating "bad" debt. Generally speaking, bad debt includes credit card debt, personal loans, car loans, and payday loans. An example of "good" debt would be a home mortgage, a small business loan, or any low-interest debt that may help you increase net worth and future income.

Not all low-interest debt is advisable; many low-interest options are attached to short-term "teaser" periods followed by much higher interest. Also, variable rates are often tied to known indexes that can quickly move up in a rising interest rate environment. A search on the internet will produce historical graphs to research index fluctuations over time. When we are in a low-interest rate environment, it all seems to work, but when that shifts, it can turn into financial hardship quickly.

Too much debt can turn good debt into bad debt in short order. Although some may disagree, I am a proponent of fixed rate obligations for good debt and not overleveraging debt obligations regardless of the category; there are few things you can't put a price tag on. Peace of mind is one of them. If the habit is set to pay cash for things versus creating bad debt, it's one less ball and chain to drag around.

In today's world, it may seem impossible to live without a credit card. I think it depends on the individual and the habits that are in place. There is no denying the benefits that certain cards carry by way of "perks" from cash back to miles for airline tickets.

Consider whether you are using credit cards for convenience or debt. If you are using your credit card for convenience and paying it off in full each month, then you are leveraging convenience, and the perks of the card are a bonus. If you struggle to pay off your credit card and have months where you carry over a balance because you spent ahead of your paycheck, put the credit cards away and use a debit card until you have a strong hold on where your money is going each month. This will ensure you have adequate reserves in place. Debit cards can be used in the same way, except the money will leave your bank account immediately. If you are using credit cards to purchase things that you will regret when the bills come, consider using a credit card for fixed expenses only, such as utility bills, gas, phone, etc.

When you make minimum payments on a credit card, you are paying interest to the bank on the amount you carry, and the next month you pay interest on the interest from the previous month. It's not beneficial to pay for dinners out and purchases you can't even remember while facing compounding credit card interest years later. You can put this money to much better use for your future goals.

Once they pay off the debt, the next step is to establish an emergency fund—a general guideline for a household with both spouses working is three months of living expenses. Specifically, I'm referring to the bills necessary for survival (rent, utilities, food, gas, etc.), rather than total expenses.

Oliver and Emma want to buy a home in three years. This is a great goal to work toward because a down payment can be daunting, especially if there isn't much disposable income. The financial planner can help them figure out what they will need to save incrementally over that time as an accumulation goal, but Oliver and Emma will need to "find" the money and figure out where they can cut back. Once dollar amounts are established to fund their monthly goals, they can decide whether to get a second part-time job; cut down on dining out, groceries, travel, etc.; or revise their goals. The ball is in their court to discuss and prioritize where their money is going each month. There are some expenses that everyone should regularly review to prevent overpaying.

Expenses to Review

CELL PHONE BILL

If you have been with the same provider for several years, you are likely paying more than you should. There are affordable options outside of the big names that we all know. Often, you will need to own your phone to transition to one of these plans, and while that may sound like a lot of money up front, you'll end up paying less in the long run. Who wants to make payments on a cell phone anyway?

CABLE BILL

How we watch TV has changed significantly in recent years. I dropped cable years ago when I realized I only watched

Hulu, Amazon, and Netflix shows. Why pay for cable? There are additional subscriptions for streaming sports and specific channels of interest such as Disney, History, etc.

INTERNET

In most households, the internet is nonnegotiable. If you haven't reviewed your plan in a while, call your internet provider and see what their current packages are. Keep in mind that they will never give you a courtesy call to let you know you are paying more than you need to be. These services have come down over the years, and it's up to you to do your homework and shop around. Also, don't rent a modem—you can buy one that pays for itself in six to eight months versus paying the rental fee forever.

AUTOMOBILE REVIEW

Not all households need two vehicles, and Emma and Oliver may find that they can survive on one. With so many employees working from home these days, many couples are moving to one car. Ideally, they will have no car debt so they can free up more cash to apply toward their other goals. A simple cost analysis can help them see what expenses are involved for each car. In addition to the monthly payment, there is also the price of gas and insurance. A hybrid or electric car for longer commutes can be economical over time.

CREDIT MONITORING

I think that everyone should subscribe to a credit-monitoring service. With identity theft being rampant, a monitoring service will alert you of inquiries and new accounts and periodically update your credit scores.

As Oliver and Emma review these areas, they may have extra money to put toward their other goals without feeling a drought of cash. To help them get organized, I would suggest they open a separate savings account for their emergency fund and a separate account for a travel fund, hobby fund, gift fund, etc. The more we can systematize through monthly deposits, the better. If you manage these accounts individually and earmark them for specific things, you know exactly how much you have to work with. Also, it may be beneficial for them to create a joint account for bills to prevent additional bank fees that add up over time.

Employee Benefits

The next step for Oliver and Emma is to review their employee benefits. While they plan to dedicate most of their extra money toward the home down payment, there are some other areas that will need to be addressed and prioritized.

At a minimum, they both should be funding their company retirement plan to take advantage of any offered match. This is free money. You put a dollar in, and they put a dollar in for you; those dollars are doubling on day one. If they want to supercharge the home goal, they can increase their retirement funds later, but they should still contribute at least up to the match amount.

Are there other benefits they are unaware of? Company perks can range from basic to comprehensive. Some of the most common are company stock in the form of RSUs (restricted stock units), ISOs (incentive stock options), NSOs (nonqualified stock options), and ESPPs (employee stock purchase programs). They all have different tax treatment, which is why it's important to have proper guidance. No one wants to end up with a large, unexpected tax bill.

There may be student loan repayment assistance, down payment assistance, etc. While rare, I have seen mortgage payment assistance programs to encourage home ownership. The bottom line is that you need to thoroughly review these programs and work with a professional to help.

Insurance Planning

There are many types of insurance out there. Although it is not the most exciting topic or category, adequate coverage is a very important component in financial planning because it can protect you, your loved ones, and your assets against unforeseen circumstances/events.

Oliver and Emma should review the following types of insurance with their planner and insurance agent regularly:

AUTO INSURANCE

Minimum coverage amounts are required, but that isn't necessarily what you should have in place. As their assets grow, coverage needs will likely change to protect what they are working hard to build.

RENTER'S INSURANCE

Oliver and Emma should have renter's insurance to protect the things inside their residence until they purchase a home.

HOMEOWNER'S INSURANCE

Once they purchase a home, an insurance agent will help them put adequate coverage in place. Many homeowners "set it and forget it," but homeowner's insurance coverage should be reviewed annually, as property values change, and change may be necessary.

LIFE INSURANCE

Term insurance: This is temporary insurance and the most inexpensive option. It is for a specific amount of time (ten, twenty, thirty years), and there is no cash value—it only pays out if you die. It's a great solution to keep the cost of insurance low and put coverage in place.

Permanent insurance: There are many permanent insurance options, all of which do not expire. Depending on how much is put into them, they can accumulate cash value inside.

DISABILITY INSURANCE

Often overlooked but extremely important, disability insurance offers comfort if a permanent disability were to cause one spouse to be unemployed. A permanent disability can wreak havoc on household finances, with one income completely disappearing and the addition of potential additional medical care expenses. There are two primary types of disability insurance.

Short-term disability (STD) insurance

Most employers provide this for all employees. STD policies will cover a disability for up to fifty-two weeks.

Long-term disability (LTD) insurance

Some employers provide coverage for employees or allow them to pay for it on their own. You can also get coverage through an outside insurance company for long-term disability. If your employer provides some but not enough to replace your income, you can supplement this with an outside policy. The benefits are tax-free if you pay the premiums, so you will not need to replace 100 percent of your income with the policy. A good rule of thumb is 70 percent. If the employer paid, they might need more because the benefits are taxable. If the employee paid, it is 100 percent tax-free, so replacement should be equivalent to their net income versus gross. Oliver and Emma should review this with the planner to ensure adequate disability coverage.

Long-term care (LTC) insurance

LTC insurance provides coverage/assistance when/if you cannot do some activities of daily living. The policies can be customized to cover varying amounts of time and benefits. Most employers do not offer this type of insurance, but if they do, make sure that it is portable (you can take it with you if you leave your employer). Oliver and Emma are too young to consider long-term care insurance, but they may want to consider this as they approach their sixties. They may have sufficient assets by that time to "self-insure" this need if they choose to, but it will be an important topic to review later.

Oliver and Emma should not delay putting adequate insurance coverage in place. As a general guideline, they should consider having coverage that equates to ten times their salary, so things like daycare and the future education of their baby will be covered. They are young and in good health; term insurance will be fairly inexpensive to put in place, which will protect them and their baby. They may have some basic coverage through work, but outside coverage is advisable—typically, companies offer one to two times the salary, which is not always enough. Also, company policies are usually not portable—if you leave the company, you can't take the policy with you. This is a problem if you become uninsurable at some point.

Investment Planning

Oliver and Emma can work with their advisor to establish a plan for the home purchase goal. They may want a more conservative investment approach for this goal because the time horizon is fairly short. On the other hand, their retirement accounts are long-term investments, and they can afford to take on more risk. Working with a financial advisor and tax professional they trust and feel comfortable with may prove very valuable in the coming years.

TAX PLANNING

Oliver and Emma should add a tax professional to their team sooner rather than later to avoid costly mistakes that they may incur if they opt to do it on their own. With constant changes in the tax code, there is peace of mind in working with someone who stays on top of the myriad of changes on an annual basis.

EDUCATION PLANNING

As a young couple with a new baby, Oliver and Emma would like to implement an education plan. They could open an account with a small monthly deposit while they save for the house or invest cash gifts for holidays/birthdays into the education account. Eleanor's grandparents may want to contribute to the education account too; it all helps and adds up over time, especially when getting an early start.

ESTATE PLANNING

Even though Oliver and Emma are just starting, areas of estate planning should be addressed, especially with a growing family. There is a misconception by many that estate planning is for the wealthy, but there are components that everyone should consider and review.

A living will, advanced directives, and a medical power of attorney

A living will and advanced directives allow us to spell out our medical treatment preferences and allow us to dictate someone to make decisions on our behalf if we are unable. Also, a will allows the naming of a guardian for their baby if something unexpected happens to them. Without this in place, the courts will make that decision for them. At a minimum, Oliver and Emma should put these documents in place with legal guidance.

A living trust

Oliver and Emma may or may not need a trust at this time. A trust is a legal entity that carries out your wishes through designated trustees after you are gone. Many employers have legal assistance available to employees to assist with basic documents. As their assets grow over time, they may want to hire an independent estate-planning attorney to review their estate plan periodically and help with any changes or updates needed.

Estate planning is unique to each individual/couple, and there are different considerations based on the state you live in. To ensure you are taking the appropriate steps, it is advisable to work with a qualified estate-planning attorney licensed in your state.

Oliver and Emma are in a great position; they both want to get organized and start on the right foot. Together they can establish a workable plan and a powerful start with a solid financial foundation.

There are many things outlined in this chapter, and it may be a little overwhelming if you are just getting started or feel that you should have started much sooner. Don't worry about getting it all done right away; the key is action. There may be one or two "easy" things that can be done right away to get momentum going.

Highlight it, dump it onto a list and prioritize, stick Post-its all over—whatever works for you. By focusing on a couple things at a time, the entire picture shapes up in no time.

Questions to Consider

→ Have you had detailed financial conversations with your spouse (or future spouse) to ensure you are on the same page?

→ Have you created a budget and guidelines to direct where your money will go and how you will handle expenses and investing for our future?

→ Are there concerns that haven't been addressed?

Do

→ Establish a plan with your spouse/partner about financial matters (ideally before marriage).

→ Bring up concerns and topics that you may be avoiding early on to establish a plan and get on the same page.

→ Be proactive and bring in professional guidance for help, if necessary.

Don't

→ Avoid conversations and postpone till next month or next year.

→ Assume things will work themselves out on their own.

→ Get defensive in these conversations. The goal is to get on the same page and establish a plan you are both comfortable with.

An initial overall review can feel like a big "to-do" list, but it becomes much more manageable when it is broken down into smaller action items. Hiring a financial advisor can add value to this process, and he/she can serve as an advocate and guide as you work toward your planning goals. Everything does not have to get done at once, and sometimes the initial list takes time to work through. Financial planning is a dynamic process. While it is important to review and make changes as necessary, it is a great sense of accomplishment to watch the progress unfold over time.

> Financial planning is a dynamic process.

Business plan

5

THE ENLIGHTENED ENTREPRENEUR

REBECCA LOOKED AROUND THE ROOM, PROUD of the decor she arranged at the last minute for the annual neighborhood Christmas party. The guests, thirty in total according to the RSVPs, should be arriving in five minutes. Ten years ago, not long after a new generation of families moved into the neighborhood, the neighbors decided that Rebecca was the ideal candidate to host the annual Christmas party, which had been a tradition for over fifty years. She didn't flinch at the opportunity to be the host, considering she loved throwing a party and had a plethora of decor she'd accumulated from her business over the years. As an interior decorator, Rebecca prided herself on creating a warm and inviting atmosphere pulled together with classic holiday decor, a place for the neighbors to be merry and share in cheer the third Saturday in December every year.

The doorbell chimed as she smoothed her palm across the red tablecloth one last time. Her husband, Evan, was still getting dressed upstairs, running behind as always.

"Don't worry. I'll get it," she said to herself.

She scanned the kitchen island that was transformed into a bar, confirming the skyline of fine wines, properly placed with labels facing outward, the shrimp tails all evenly spaced along the rim of the cocktail-filled martini glasses.

It didn't take long for Rebecca's kitchen to be filled with the neighborhood couples, all dressed in shades of red and green. Along the main wall, two tables were covered in themed appetizers and beverages, a steady flow of guests filled their plates while mingling. Conversations punched the air, marked by an ongoing ripple of laughter that spilled into the adjoining rooms where guests had trickled to.

Three years ago, Rebecca had learned that it was beneficial to hire additional help during these parties so she could socialize while the food, beverages, and cleaning were tended to. Grateful for the free time, she walked over to a cluster of guests who were engaged in what appeared to be a deep conversation. Just when she heard talk of finance, she spun on her heel and started to walk away toward a more interesting chat, but she stopped midstride when a question was directed at her.

"How's the interior decorating business going?" The inquiry came from a neighbor who had always been attentive to Rebecca's artsy business.

Happy that he had switched gears in the conversation, Rebecca was always eager to talk about the career she loved. "Oh, it's great. This time of year, of course, is always pretty busy, but I can't complain." She took a sip of the signature cocktail she designed herself, the sweetness of the cranberry juice offset by the sprig of mint that was dangling off the lip of the glass. "And how is the construction business?"

"Slow right now, but thankfully I budget for that every year," he said, as a modest grin tugged at his lips.

"Cheers to that." Evan entered the conversation, raising a cocktail glass in toast. "What are we talking about?" His question conjured a ripple of laughter from the circle of guests.

"Budgeting ... you know all that fun adult talk." Jeff, a successful real estate agent who lived directly next door to Rebecca and Evan, added. "It took me a while to learn how to actually budget for my business with all the highs and lows involved in real estate, but once I got the hang of it, it all made sense, and we feel a heck of a lot more at ease."

Rebecca had never had much downtime since she'd been an interior decorator. Sure, the business had its ups and downs like all businesses do, but she never had a long drought of zero income, like the winter months for construction workers. Thankfully, Evan made a steady living as an engineer, and they could rely on his regular paychecks. But what if Evan lost his job and their family of four had to survive solely on her income? All she did with her money was keep it in a checking account. In the past, Evan had suggested that she meet with someone to help her with organizing the business, but she avoided it, overwhelmed by the thought of what might be uncovered.

"What does that look like?" Rebecca felt ashamed for asking the question. She should know how to budget money by now. She was in her midforties and had been running her business for ten years. "I mean, budgeting as a solo business owner? How do you do that?"

Her words came out with less confidence than she intended, and for the first time in a long time she felt like she was missing out on something. What if everyone was saving their money the right way, and privy to all the proper ways of investing, and she was the only one doing it wrong? The more she thought about it, the smaller she felt. She scanned the room and found herself feeling heavy with shame. Everyone seemed to have their financial situation figured out.

"The retirement calculator shows us having enough when Evan retires, so my money just serves as a backup plan." As she said the words, it all became clear to her. She hadn't given much thought to her own income and assumed that Evan's investments would be plentiful for the both of them when they retired. Until this moment, the idea of maximizing her income wasn't a consideration, and they had relied solely on Evan's salary to do the work for them. In the past, Evan had expressed his apprehension about having to carry the family's financial weight, but his content and laid-back personality often left the concern unattended.

"Well, I guess you have to ask yourself how the four of you would survive if something happened to Evan." Jeff dropped the words between them matter-of-factly, but they left behind a heavy weight on Rebecca's shoulders. "I'd be happy to share some of the tools I've implemented with my own business."

"I'd appreciate that. That would be great." Rebecca plucked an hors d'oeuvre from a tray being passed around and bit into the puffed pastry; the savory blend of spices and cheese created a welcoming flavor that washed away the bitterness of her financial worries.

What's Rebecca's Money Narrative?

Financial planning always comes down to the same three variables: what we spend, what we earn, and how much we save. When the numbers are not adding up, we must decrease or increase one of those variables.

In this situation, it's clear that Rebecca takes pride in her business as an interior decorator. She is current on industry trends in her business and has a passion for creating beautiful living spaces.

> Financial planning always comes down to the same three variables: what we spend, what we earn, and how much we save.

The financial aspects of Rebecca's business seem to be at the bottom of her priority list. Whether you are a landscaper, a hairdresser, or an interior decorator, your main goal is to bring in new clients at a steady pace. With all the focus on growth, it's easy for self-employed business owners to forego addressing the additional responsibilities of running a business.

Unlike a corporate job, where employees fall under an umbrella of rules, handbooks, and professionals to guide them along the way, the self-employed business owner is on an island, untethered to all the privileges and options that a large company offers. There is no one encouraging you to contribute to a 401(k), go for that promotion, or set up a direct deposit for savings and college plans. And there are no fellow colleagues to chat with around the water cooler about financial tips.

There are many rewards involved in self-employment and the goal of building a successful business. Many pursue this in the hope of more freedom, fulfilling a dream, and additional control over decisions. Still, it also comes with additional roles and responsibilities that can wreak havoc on a business if avoided.

I have been self-employed most of my career and can empathize with Rebecca's situation. When I first branched off and opened my own mortgage office, I felt like I was on an episode of *Survivor*; there was no handbook that came with my freshly signed lease, and I quickly realized how much I didn't know. I underestimated the value (and cost) of someone else worrying about the printers, computers, phone system, marketing, etc. I was equipped with product knowledge and my client base, but I didn't have a handle on how to run the business itself.

Self-doubt crept in quickly. I was ambitious but also realistic when it came to the bleak statistics surrounding the success of new businesses. Similar to learning how to ride my little motorcycle, I became more comfortable over time, and as one challenge subsided, new ones emerged.

Through personal experience and working with many other small business owners, there are some areas of organization that are more challenging than others. There are some responsibilities that are easier to solve that fall under HR and finance: bookkeeping, payroll, taxes, benefits, IT, etc. These tasks are fairly simple to outsource and delegate to other professionals. The other categories can be a bit more challenging: sales, marketing, customer service and retention, research, etc. The subcategories can vary based on the industry. In a larger company structure, there are departments for these categories. For a solo entrepreneur or small business, there can be many "gaps" that require the business owners to step into roles that are not their strong suit or engage in tasks that they have never done before. You can't walk down the hall and hand the task to the suitable department because *you* are *all* departments. Another thing to note is that when you do hire an additional employee, they are typically required to wear many hats too. Awareness is key in finding solutions to fill some of these gaps as you grow, or you may find yourself wasting a lot of time on things that are not in your natural wheelhouse, which can significantly impact your growth goals/projections, stress, and burnout.

The first step is an authentic self-assessment of your strengths and weaknesses as it relates to your various roles and responsibilities. Many business owners succeed at self-managing, whereas many fail. If you find that you avoid working *on* the business versus *in* it, it is important to build a solid financial team to ensure that you are doing all you can to protect yourself and the business while also planning.

Adding professionals to your "executive" team is important as you grow. It is often hard for self-employed people to divide the income of the business as a whole and their own personal income, and the sooner those two are divided, the better.

I get it. When you are in the early stages of building a business, it's easy to get lost in the growth of expanding your clientele. However, let's take a step back and look at some of the core items you need to have established if you want to maintain and protect what you are working hard to build.

There are many ways to structure a business: sole proprietor, LLC, S Corp, C Corp, etc. A good financial advisor and tax professional can help with the appropriate structure. It may be tempting at the start to funnel all your money into one account and draw from it, but this can be very confusing from a planning perspective because you won't know how much net revenue you are pulling in. In other words, you need to keep tabs on the income that ends up in your pocket, which is why a separation of the various streams of income is important.

The easiest way to think of it is that when you are self-employed, you are wearing two hats: one as the employer (of yourself) and one as the employee. This can be a little confusing because they are technically the same person. When you put your employer hat on, you need to make sure that you are doing all you can to ensure success for the business, which can include how the business is structured, vision and growth plans, marketing, sufficient protection for unforeseeable events, looking out for your staff (employees), and compensation to yourself as a business owner.

When you put on your "employee" hat, there are different considerations. Imagine that you are an employee and you're working for someone else. Would you stay or would you quit? Are you properly compensated for your role? How much would it cost to hire someone to take over your duties as an employee of your business? Small business owners often wear many hats and have trouble with this. We all have our unique strengths and weaknesses—know what you are good at and build a team to help with the other areas.

After Rebecca meets with an advisor, she may discover that she is not earning nearly as much as she thought, considering expenses were coming from the income to the business, which is not income to her. If her money seems to be disappearing, the answer could be that her expenses are much higher than she realizes, leaving very little that is passing through as personal income. For a hobby business, that may be okay, but it's clear that Rebecca is trying to earn income for her family by building a profitable business. Otherwise, she'd likely be allocating her time differently.

We also know that Rebecca loves what she does. While the passion component is important for any business owner, in some cases it can be a detriment to growth. She may find herself taking time on projects because she is focusing on the sheer joy of doing them while not sticking to the deadlines that would be in place within a larger organization.

By setting deadlines for herself and overall checks and balances, she will put structure in place that will allow her to monitor progress and growth. Another consideration is opportunity cost: How much is she losing by running her own business versus what she would earn if she worked for someone else? Suppose she was earning $100,000 at her previous job and has been breaking even for ten years with her own business. In that case, that is a significant income that she didn't receive over that time frame, which could shift her overall perspective and nudge her to put timelines and growth goals in place.

Rebecca should consider thoroughly reviewing her business income, expenses, and previous tax returns to see where she stands. Next, she can establish separate bank accounts, one for the design business and one for personal use. All business expenses should be run through the business account. Each month, a personal draw (salary) should go from her business account to her personal account (even if it is just a transfer online). She could research salary averages for lead designers in her area to determine how much this number should be. Out of the personal account, she can work with her husband and the planner to allocate this money toward household expenses, retirement, and savings goals, along with discretionary spending goals such as vacations and hobbies. Additionally, she should review self-employed retirement plan options with the planner and put a goal in place to establish a plan that will allow her to contribute as an employee and as an employer as revenue increases.

At the end of each year, business financials should be reviewed, and surplus profits can be drawn as a bonus to her as the business owner. If there is not enough to fund her personal salary, she can see how much she is really earning in the business and revise her plan and structure going forward. This will create clarity if there are revisions needed for the business plan, such as raising fees to increase revenue, but to address all of this, she needs to know what her numbers are now.

Rebecca and Evan can look at the entire picture and ensure they are on the same page with financial planning for their family. Rebecca cannot assume that Evan maxing out his retirement options at work will satisfy the gap for them to retire. As an example, the planner may conclude that they need to save an additional 20 percent of their gross income to retire with the lifestyle they want. While this may be difficult to accept, at least they know what is needed to reach their goals. The good news is that they have decades to make positive changes. If they continue to put this off, the window closes each year with less time to make changes and turn things around. By lifting the blankets on their finances, it will allow them to make major shifts by creating a game plan, and these positive changes will spill over into their marriage, their children, and their future.

It's important to add that not all business owners should be business owners. The desire to start a business often stems from the idea that there is more freedom in your working hours; however, it can be the opposite. Business owners don't punch in and punch out, and they are often victims to their wheels constantly spinning and fulfilling many roles until there is revenue to hire others to fill the gaps. It takes additional discipline to manage a business. Many self-employed workers spend a good amount of their time playing "catch-up" because their income is received in chunks that they use to pay off debt or taxes incurred from the previous unpaid months. Real estate agents often fall into this trap since transactions can come in waves with dry spells in between.

Catching up is not fun; the goal is to get ahead of the planning and be realistic about the ups and downs throughout the year. Businesses need reserves to accommodate the way revenue ebbs and flows. When checks come in, the money should be immediately distributed to the appropriate buckets for taxes and reserves (salaries, business expenses, etc.). It takes discipline to move from catching up to getting ahead.

Differentiating your roles as the employer and employee is important. You would not join a company and work for free, right? Many business owners work for free year after year for themselves. This is fairly normal initially, but it must have timelines and parameters around it.

Sometimes all it takes is a passing conversation at a party to change the path of your finances. While it was scary for Rebecca to decide to take a closer look at her business, the important thing is that she decided to act on it. She may find that things aren't as bad as she thought, or the opposite may be true. Either way, she can create an updated plan for her business and family's financial future.

Questions to Consider

→ Are you managing your personal and business finances separately?

→ Do you have advisors in place who identify gaps and opportunities and assist with changes as necessary?

→ If you are considering starting a business, have you written down all of the additional responsibilities you will have as a business owner as you consider making the change?

Do

→ Research and identify additional expenses, responsibilities, and opportunities before embarking on a new business venture.

→ Regularly review your numbers (if you are already in business) and seek assistance and guidance as needed to identify gaps and opportunities.

→ Recognize your strengths and weaknesses as a business owner so that you can add support as you grow in areas that can be delegated.

→ Separate business and personal bank accounts and credit lines for ease of planning and transparency.

Don't

→ Eliminate the opportunity cost and value of your time spent on the business and in the business when reviewing your numbers.

→ Put off adding a benefits package for yourself for an extended period of time. If cash flow consistently doesn't allow for this, an evaluation and deadline should be in place to continue growing the business or move on to something different.

→ Be afraid to seek help with business planning. There are many additional considerations, and a good financial team can make all the difference in how you manage revenue and grow.

6

THE SANDWICH GENERATION

THE WILLOW SCHOOL AUDITORIUM WAS PACKED with spectators, eagerly awaiting the spring concert. It was a time for students to show off the music skills they had been refining all year long, and Beth and Zack were always delighted to watch their son Mason do what he did best: lead a group of students in song. This year was particularly exciting because their grandson would be one of the soloists.

"Did you ever think our son would be leading a group of kids on a stage?" Zack bumped Beth's elbow as the chatter of the hall reached an all-time high with last-minute attendees trying to find their seats.

Now that she thought about it, Beth could always picture Mason on a stage leading children. At a young age, he'd picked up on a natural talent for anything musical, and he was always able to relate to kids on a level most were not.

"Actually, yes, I did picture him in this exact role on more than one occasion," she said, as her gaze caught a boy's round face peeking behind the corner of the curtain.

"Hey there, neighbors, are these seats taken?" Beth looked up to see their younger neighbors with their three children in tow. The siblings were already bickering about having to waste their evening watching their younger brother on stage.

"They're all yours," Zack said as he continued the conversation with Beth. "Really? I don't know. I guess I always had hopes that he'd follow through with his dream of being a lawyer. Where did that dream go anyway?"

Before Beth could answer, she felt a surge of resentment run through her body. She loved her son more than anything in the world. It's why she and Zack had sacrificed so much for him. They wanted to give him a chance that they didn't have growing up. As their only child, they put their all into his upbringing and had no qualms about paying for a pricey private school education, followed by a prestigious New England university following high school. Halfway through his college career, he decided that law school wasn't the right fit, and he switched his major to music, following the passion that he had always latched on to. "I guess he decided to focus on his first love."

"Thankfully music makes him some money. Had I followed my dream of becoming a professional baseball player, I'm not sure you'd be sitting next to me right now," Zack said, winking at his wife.

"You were a good ball player," Beth said, remembering the days when they first met. Zack had been a good player, but both of them knew what it was like to grow up without money, and they made it their mission to focus on careers that pulled in bigger salaries than their own parents' jobs. And as a result, Mason was on the receiving end of their hard work and generosity. They never wanted to see their boy go without or be strapped with the stress of surmounting debt, which is why they agreed, without a second thought, to take on student loans to fund his education. And the pride they felt when Mason's good grades landed him an acceptance letter to a top-notch college seemed to diminish all thoughts of Beth and Zack having to pay back those loans.

"Well, maybe I'll pick it up again when we retire," Zack said, letting out a jovial laugh.

Lately, the thought of retirement was something that brought with it a sick feeling in the pit of Beth's stomach. Her husband always had a glass-half-full outlook on life, and it was one of the traits that she loved most about him, but it often caused him to struggle with looking at the reality of a situation. As a bookkeeper for a financial firm, Beth had been the one to manage the finances in their marriage, seldom sharing where they were with their financial situation.

At sixty years old, she had spent her life dreaming of a retirement that was marked by trips to destinations they'd never been and a second home, a Vermont cabin where they could tend to a handful of animals they'd always wanted. But she didn't have the heart to tell Zack just how much they still owed on Mason's debt. She also hadn't told him about the hefty price tag that was attached to the assisted living facility she and her sisters had selected for their aging mother. While her mother had some money left in retirement and savings, it wasn't enough to cover the price of assisted living, and if they wanted to keep up with both the college debt and their mother's living situation, Beth knew deep down inside that the couple might have to sell the home they had never planned on leaving.

"Aah … I can't wait until I punch the time clock the last time. Then it will just be me and you, babe," Zack said, bumping elbows with Beth. Avoiding the topic of retirement, Beth settled into her seat and allowed her son's music to calm her nerves.

When the show was over, Zack and Beth raced to the stage where their neighbors were doling out congratulatory hugs. Mason, as always, was surrounded by parents praising him for a job well done. Beth felt pride bubble up inside her as she watched her son on the receiving end of so much admiration. For a brief moment, it concealed some of the emotionally draining worries she'd been having about their futures. Mason was living proof that dreams could be achieved, but deep down inside she felt like she could've gone about his college debt differently. All she could think about was how proud she was that her son had gotten into a prestigious school, and she never took into consideration what those college loans would do to her and Zack's retirement. On top of that, the bills for her mother's assisted living facility would be adding up soon.

"Do you ever feel like we are living for everyone but ourselves?" Beth eased into the conversation with Zack on their drive home from the show.

"How so?" he asked as he turned onto their street. Beth recognized how all the front lawns had recently sprung to life, showing off their vibrant greens from the recent spring showers.

"Well, who knows how long we're going to be paying for Mason's education, and my mother's living expenses are through the roof."

"Well, maybe Mason can start helping out. I mean, he does have tenure at the school now." Zack said the words matter-of-factly, as if they had always been sitting on the tip of his tongue waiting to be expressed.

Beth nearly gasped. She'd taken so much pride in making sure her son was taken care of that she never thought about asking him to pay for his education. "We can't do that!"

"We raised an amazing kid. I think we owe it to him to be honest about what we can do to help and where he needs to contribute."

What's Zack and Beth's Money Narrative?

As parents, we want what's best for our children. And it's beyond rewarding when we're able to present our children with opportunities so they can pursue their goals in a way that we were never able to. When we put our own financial health in jeopardy to do this, we aren't doing our children any favors. Much in the same way we are told to put our oxygen masks on before our child's on an airplane, it's a good idea to put ourselves first financially. And then, we can let our successes trickle down so we can help others.

> Much in the same way we are told to put our oxygen masks on before our child's on an airplane, it's a good idea to put ourselves first financially.

Back in the day, it was common for children to move their parents in with them when they got older. This allowed them to take care of them and avoid the high price of assisted living homes. However, times have changed, and this joint living situation is no longer a given. Many family members who take on the role of caretaker simply aren't skilled or prepared for the additional magnitude of responsibility. As the level of care increases, family members who are acting as caretakers can't assess or see when they are in over their head.

When my kids were little, I felt tired all the time. This was *physical* exhaustion from being up half the night and running around after them. When they became teenagers, I felt *emotionally* exhausted. Financial decisions can similarly be emotionally exhausting when tied to those we love.

If your five-year-old repeatedly asks for candy, it is easy to say no, right? Because it is clearly unhealthy for them, they can get cavities, and you know it will keep them up all night. As they get older, they might ask for ten toys every time you walk into a store. Again, you say no because you want them to appreciate the things they have and grow up with values and good principles. From a financial perspective, would it be a hardship to buy these things for your child? Five candy bars or ten cheap toys don't really cost that much. It's not about the money.

So, what happens when it is about the money? Zack and Beth have worked tirelessly to provide things they didn't have—this is emotional. But it has a hefty price tag. If they were at the toy store and the ask for the ten toys was not just about overindulging but also that they wouldn't be able to pay their mortgage, that would be a simple, hard no. Because that's crazy, right? But for some reason, that perspective can be lost when the ramifications of financial decisions today don't come until later. If we focus on our overall long-term health regarding financial decisions similar to the candy bar, the decisions become easier. If I pay for the pricey private school that I can't afford, it will create additional stress and future financial problems for our household that will affect all of us negatively.

The term "sandwich generation" was prevalent for Zack and Beth, as they were smack in the middle of two major financial commitments that had the potential to alter their future drastically. No one wants to burden their children down the road, which is why financial independence is so important.

$ $ $

They aren't alone, as this generation currently makes up a quarter of the US population, and many are faced with similar challenges. When it came to Mason's student debt, they had planned on paying it off with income and bonuses, but life most likely got in the way. Oftentimes, economic shifts and employment changes over the years have the capacity to derail a couple's future plans. Zack and Beth may be "slowing down" and don't have the energy they once did to take on sixteen-hour days or a second job, which can make earning extra money on the side more difficult.

Beth and Zack have some big decisions to make, which could have a major impact on their financial future. They can continue to brush all of this under the rug, or they can take a hard look at the situation and make some changes.

First, they need to get on the same page as a couple and lay everything on the table. Zack shouldn't be in the dark about the debt or the care expenses associated with Beth's mother. It isn't fair to either of them. They can't begin to shift their situation until they do this, whether they decide to tackle their finances on their own or recruit the help of an outside professional.

Once they are aligned as a couple, they can discuss the situation with Mason. While it is understandably hard to transition from viewing your kids as kids to accepting them as young adults, Zack and Beth aren't doing their son any favors by leaving him in the dark. They may also need to have a similar conversation with Beth's mom. I know they want what is best for her, but they shouldn't put themselves in financial ruin over it. If Beth's mom has no assets of her own, she may be eligible for Medicaid to assist with the cost of care.

Zack and Beth may need outside guidance to sort through their current position and move forward. With some shifts now, they can work toward helping Mason and Beth's mom without bankrupting themselves.

The good news is there is still time to make some positive changes. They are both still working and can make a big difference in the future by addressing it now.

Questions to Consider

➔ Are you regularly reviewing your personal financial plan to ensure you are on track for your goals?

➔ Are other expenses potentially putting your financial future in jeopardy?

➔ Are there areas where emotions may be taking over logic with your financial decisions?

Do

→ Have conversations with your partner/family members to express concern without judgment.

→ Write down a "to-do" list to research costs for all options versus guess estimates.

→ Seek professional guidance for assistance if necessary.

Don't

→ Ignore a problem that could become a bigger one over time.

→ Panic about a potential situation; focus on gathering all the facts and options.

→ Make dramatic changes before you receive a second (and possibly third) opinion.

College planning and caring for elderly parents will impact the majority of people at some point in their lives. Like other financial planning topics, the earlier we address the goal and create a plan, the better. If you are young and just starting out, you are in the ideal position to attack these goals early; additional years add additional ease in achieving financial goals. If you are older and these challenges are coming up, there is still hope. Now is always better than later, and every year counts. In comparison, it is like being little and afraid of the dark. When the sun comes up in the morning and we can see under the bed and into the closet, things aren't nearly as frightening.

7

THE BROKE MILLIONAIRE

PAIGE WAS BORN WITH BUILT-IN MOTIVATION AND drive. If challenged, she accepted. Not only did she accept, but she went above and beyond with everything—especially money. It was no surprise that she was a top saleswoman for her company, pulling in a record-breaking seven figures steadily for the last ten years. After all, she put in the long hours and hard work that are often required of sales reps, and her perseverance paid off when she was awarded the top sales accolades on a national level.

She was the breadwinner in her family, and that was no secret, considering she made it her mission to top the list at her firm year after year, which came with top-producer perks and awards at company conferences. Everyone knew Paige made the bucks—except Paige. She was never quite happy with her earning status and was constantly attempting ways to acquire more cash, striving to be better than she already was, which was an incredibly hard feat to tackle. Paige and her family live in a multimillion-dollar home in the heart of one of the priciest cities in America. Her children attend a prestigious private school, and she has a vacation home that seldom gets used.

It wasn't rare for Paige to show up at her friend Abby's house, fired up about her lack of money. "I need to make more money. My accounts aren't reflecting what I want." She sat on the edge of the seat, unable to sit still and fueled by her desire to have more.

Abby raised an eyebrow and tilted her head. "Paige, you push yourself to increase your income year after year and always do. Where is it all going?"

"Yes, but why am I still so broke? I make more money than nearly everyone I know according to the data that is spilled all over the business magazines, but I have nothing to show for it."

"Well, let's see. You own two properties in high cost-of-living areas, both of your children attend private schools, and I've seen how stressed you've been," Abby said as she handed Paige a cup of tea and dropped onto the couch.

"I don't know. I guess I feel like I want my family and I to have the things my husband and I didn't have growing up. There were no family vacations, no brand names. I never had a new outfit in high school; everything was hand-me-downs or bought at Goodwill." Paige paused, remembering how she felt when she was the only one of her friends not wearing Gap jeans, a memory that still stung. "I guess I just want more for my children."

As they continued to talk, Abby learned that she had many layers to peel about what was going on in her friend's life. The first one was glaringly obvious. Paige enjoyed spending money more than she enjoyed earning it, and as her income grew, her spending increased. As if it was artfully planned out, her earnings managed to be one step behind her spending at all times. Interestingly, Paige shared that her dad had a similar mindset. Much like Paige's husband, Owen, her mom was always happy with a simpler life and a job she enjoyed without much regard to income or what she could be earning. Her dad, on the other hand, took big risks that put the family into financial hardship more than once. While her mother spent time and mental energy pinching pennies, her father would throw years of this progress away by attaching their finances to a "big idea" that would set them back substantially. Owen had grown up with two parents who were both poor money managers, and finances became a source of tension and fear for him growing up, so he unknowingly enabled Paige by letting her handle all the money matters.

"Do you feel like you need to have all these things to make you happy?"

A wave of honesty crashed over Paige. "I guess I thought I did, but the truth is … I spend so much time working and stressed over bringing in money that I can never even enjoy the things we have." She dropped her head in her hands. "None of this brings me anything other than bills. And we have a second home we bought for vacations, and we never use it. It just sits there." Waving her hand around the room as if she was referring to Abby's living room space as the culprit, she shook her head as her confession hit her, a light bulb moment revealing its magic.

Paige began to think more about all of this and realized the emotions that were driving her were not producing the results she wanted, and things needed to change. She shared some of this with Owen, and right away he was very supportive. Together they became determined to figure out what was really going on, and they set out on a mission to acquire some help for the well-being of their marriage, family, and future. Owen didn't like seeing Paige so stressed all the time, but he didn't know how to fix it. There was an air of relief and excitement as they began these conversations, and they both began to see their priorities shifting immediately. Abby took it a step further and referred them to a financial advisor she knew, and they set up an appointment right away.

What's Paige's Money Narrative?

Paige's situation has *nothing* to do with money—she makes plenty. It also has nothing to do with being financially savvy overall. She reads financial papers and watches the news every day, so she is "in the know." It's more about deep-rooted habits and beliefs.

> Every dollar of added income triggers her desire for a new expense. It's time for a total reset.

The good news is this is a fairly easy problem to fix, as long as there is commitment. But the only person who can fix it is Paige. There is plenty of money to work with, and the issue is 100 percent about resetting habits. Every dollar of added income triggers her desire for a new expense. It's time for a total reset.

Paige makes more money than the average American dreams of, yet she was living paycheck to paycheck. Hard to believe, right? Unfortunately, this scenario is more common than you might think. If I went through her bank statement with a fine-tooth comb, I'd be able to gain more insight into where things weren't adding up. Most of their money is likely going to mortgages, property taxes, and private tuition.

If Paige is a risk taker *and* a big spender, she would naturally be on a mental hamster wheel of constantly striving to make more and not giving anything up. And what that is doing is creating a level of anxiety and stress that could be damaging to her health. Many in this situation are so focused on making more money that they miss out on other things that bring them joy and happiness without price tags attached.

It comes down to budgeting guidelines. Oftentimes, people who spend too much and live paycheck to paycheck simply aren't living within their guidelines. Paige is a perfect example of someone who should have firmer boundaries attached to her spending. I'm a fan of the 50/30/20 budget rule, which provides a guide that establishes whether income and expenses are aligned in a healthy way. The 50/30/20 budget rule breaks down like this: 50 percent of your money goes toward needs or essentials, 30 percent goes toward wants, and 20 percent goes toward savings.

For the 50 percent that goes toward needs, you might include mortgage payments, rent, property taxes, insurance premiums, groceries, healthcare, utilities, and gas. Many would also include minimum credit card debt payments under the 50 percent umbrella, but I am not a fan of carrying any debt outside of what is paid off each month and falls within the three categories.

Thirty percent goes toward the wants—if you have credit card debt, your wants money should go toward paying it off first. Wants include nonessentials such as dinners out, travel, accessories, hobbies, subscriptions, etc.

Twenty percent goes toward savings/investments—this should be the amount that is dedicated to building your emergency reserves first, then funding retirement and investment accounts.

If Paige and Owen find that housing expenses and tuition are above the 50 percent threshold, they will need to discuss and assess how to get this number below 50 percent. This could mean that they have to downsize their primary home, sell the vacation property, or rent it out, as well as looking at other education options for the kids.

The budget rule is a broad overview, and for many people it helps to take those needs and wants buckets and break them down further, simplifying the process by divvying expenses up into "buckets" based on priorities. By dedicating "buckets" of money for taxes, expenses and entertainment, vacations, and home projects, it makes saving seem less mentally strenuous, because everything is accounted for. I would also advise Paige to consider selling the unused vacation property if it is creating additional expenses and tying up resources that could be allocated elsewhere.

These tools will offer a healthy, stress-free way of saving money, allowing Paige, Owen, and their children to actually enjoy the things they purchased. Instead of letting their money control them in a reactive way, it is time they told their money where to go. Resetting old habits isn't always easy, but once you get a good stride, things can fall into place fairly quickly. Eventually, when you stop thinking about your past decisions and start focusing on what you can change in the future, things will fall into place.

Both Paige and Owen can shift their money narrative and create a happier, more peaceful life, which their children will naturally pick up on.

It's admirable that Paige wants to provide so much for her family and those closest to her. While her work ethic is inspiring and it's a generous act to want to give her children things she didn't grow up with, it's coming at a price that might not be worth it, taking a toll on her both mentally and physically.

Questions to Consider

→ Do you feel you have a good understanding about where your money is going each month?

→ Are you living within a 50/30/20 budget guideline?

→ Do you feel like you are catching up more often than feeling ahead or on top of your monthly finances?

Do

→ Review your income, expenses, and cash flow one to two times per year to monitor and update changes.

→ Consider applying variable bonuses and "extra" income toward goals versus increasing expenses.

→ Consider additional guidance if you need help analyzing your overall picture.

Don't

→ Incur additional debt to keep up with increasing expenses.

→ Count on discretionary bonuses and income for fixed expenses.

→ Avoid addressing the situation if you feel overwhelmed and stressed out. There may be some simple adjustments to shift things in a positive direction.

More money can often seem like the solution to life's problems. In some cases, this is true. If you are in a career where you are not earning a livable wage relative to the area you live in, if you are a single parent with a lot of responsibility and doing all that you can, have a partner/spouse who struggles to hold a job or is unwilling to work, or have experienced tragedy beyond your control, there are circumstances and situations that are hard, and I don't want to minimize that.

In other situations, when income continues to increase and lifestyle expenses rise at a greater pace while dollars disappear, it likely has more to do with overall habits than the need for more money. The stress and angst of living like that is not worth sacrificing peace of mind and living within your means. Although letting go might initially seem like surrender, it can be empowering. Reflecting and assessing your situation can provide a valuable reset, enabling you to position yourself for greater growth than staying on your current path.

8

LESSONS IN COLLECTIONS

FTER A LONG, STRESSFUL DAY AT THE OFFICE, where he ran a real estate and property management business for the past twenty-five years, Nick let out a sigh of relief as he stepped into his garage. It had been a space he had expanded over the years to support his growing car collection. Surrounding him were the gleaming bodies of the vehicles he'd given new life to. He ran a palm along the cool hood of a white 1953 Corvette Roadster, proud of the work he had put into it. While most of the fixer-upper duties were completed by professional mechanics that he hired, he had learned a thing or two in the process. At least, now he could change the oil and do a basic tune-up.

Nick's interest in cars started when he was only eight years old, when he spent summer afternoons helping his uncle, Frankie, wax his own collection. It never failed. The smell of the wax and engine oil always brought Nick back to those summers, accompanied by a wave of comfort from moments spent with the man he admired so much. The rest of his family often joked about how similar Nick and Frankie were, and thus a bond was formed. Over cars. Now, in addition to the nostalgia he experienced from waxing his own cars, he loved driving them around on the weekends, and as an added bonus, he received applause for their picture-perfect condition.

Nick's love of antique vehicles only grew after Uncle Frankie gifted him with one of his cars, spurring a hobby that would last a lifetime. Now, looking down at the hood of the car, Nick saw the reflection of a moving silhouette. He spun around to see his teenage son, Christopher.

"Hey, Dad." The boy leaned on a Buick Chevelle.

"Hey, Bud, what's up?" Nick said, as he headed toward the tub of wax and started going to work spinning the cloth in circles on the rear of the corvette.

In a true teenage response, Christopher didn't answer. Instead, he started asking his father questions. "I don't get it, Dad. Why do you spend so much time with these cars in the garage?"

"What do you mean?" Nick, genuinely confused, paused midspin and looked up.

"I mean, why do you spend so much time on *this*?" Christopher stretched his arms out into one wide wingspan and spun around once. "Why do you collect these cars? You hardly ever use them, and we're not even allowed to touch them."

"I'm letting you touch one now, aren't I?" Nick lifted his chin in the direction of where Christopher was leaning on the hood.

But the inquiry pinched at his guilt. Why was he spending so much money on these vehicles that only got used in the warmer months? Half of the year, he simply admired them. It filled him with immense joy, but the realistic side of his mind was asking the same question that his impressionable son was asking. "Well, I guess it brings me joy."

"Aren't there other hobbies that won't take up so much time and space so I can at least fit my bike in the garage?" Christopher leaned back further on the hood, and Nick stopped himself before he lectured his son on the hazards of denting the vehicle. It was no secret that he was protective of his collection, but he tried to keep it under wraps the best he could.

"I'm pretty sure Dan's dad collects stamps and old toys. I mean, that doesn't require such maintenance and upkeep as these cars do. And they don't take up nearly as much room and cost way less." Christopher looked around the garage, a space that had been greatly expanded since he acquired his first vintage car all those years ago. He would have to rent garage space if he continued to collect.

"True." Nick thought about ways to use this exchange as a teaching moment. "It's kind of like how you used to collect G.I. Joe figures. Remember how excited you would get when a new one came out?"

Christopher rolled his eyes. "Yeah, but I was like seven." He pushed himself upright and ambled out of the garage and back into the house.

The conversation was over, but Nick's guilt remained. He did spend an awful lot of money and time on these things. He was always fixing something on one of the cars and had a wish list of refurbished old stock parts he always had an eye out for. The engine work was endless—it seemed like once something was fixed, something else would break. Much of his hobby money was spent on the long list of people he had to hire to keep his cars gleaming. The only thing he did himself was clean the upholstery and polish the body. Painters were paid to apply the finishing touches to the exterior, as were high-priced engine mechanics who knew the ins and outs of these old beauties.

He dropped the cloth on the car and hunkered into the chair by his tool bench. A sense of guilt creeped up on him like it had in the past, when others made jokes about the mini fortune he had put into his hobby. He thought about how his wife liked to knit and crochet, but the expenses seemed minimal compared to his car collection. Nick loved getting lost in his cars after a long week at work. While vastly different, they each supported one another's hobbies, and this was shown in the many gifts they purchased throughout the year. One of

Nick's favorite ornaments was a red vintage Corvette with his name personalized on the mini license plate. He remembered how his wife smiled slyly at the secret ornament she hung on his tool bench, leaving it for him to find one Christmas Eve while he showed off his newest projects to visiting family members. She made it clear that she loved taking weekend rides in the cars just as much as he did.

Nick felt a wave of confusion over the feelings that were surging through him. Why did he have this nagging guilt about spending money on the hobby he loved so much? He thought about how his own father rarely spent money on himself, and that was quickly pushed aside with a rationalization. The value of his cars had nearly kept up with what he spent, even though he knew he'd never sell them. His hobby had never been at the expense of his family's financial goals— they had managed to save and invest at least 25 percent of everything they made during their entire marriage. He was on track to retire much earlier than they had planned if he wanted to, but he enjoyed running the real estate business. So, why did he find himself slipping into feelings of guilt?

What's Nick's Money Narrative?

It's hard to say where Nick's feelings are coming from, but I think consumption guilt or regret is something many of us can relate to at some point in our lives. Nick's parents may have passed on their own feelings around spending; babies of the Great Depression were all too familiar with scarcity and frugality for survival. Or Nick may have personally endured financial struggles in his past and has a deep fear of being in the same position again.

Nick has worked hard to be in a stable financial position, and there is nothing wrong with having an expensive hobby, as long as he can afford it. Based on what we can see about Nick and his family, they are ahead of their goals and on the right path. If Nick was in debt over his hobby and sacrificing other goals to work on the cars, that would be a cause for concern.

> Building solid financial habits should be fun and ultimately free you to do *more* of the things you enjoy doing.

Financial planning can sometimes be attached to the notion that you must always strive to spend less and save more, and that is not always the case. Sometimes, the opposite is true.

Building solid financial habits should be fun and ultimately free you to do *more* of the things you enjoy doing. By creating goals and timelines for directing your money, you set the wheels in motion to stay on track for long-term success. In turn, you can use discretionary funds for whatever you want—vacations, gifts, entertainment, hobbies—free of guilt.

I am personally a collector of many things; some have more value than others, and some would have minimal value to anyone else but me. I love to think about who owned things a century ago, what it was used for, and the value it holds in history.

During the COVID-19 pandemic, I bought a massive collection of four hundred typewriters. In hindsight, I don't know what I was thinking. I had three typewriters in my collection at the time. It seemed like a fun adventure, and I figured I could hire someone to help sell the majority of them quickly, recover the investment, and keep the ones I really wanted to fix up over time and move on. Well, turning typewriters over is no small feat—some are extremely heavy, and it's not easy to pack them up and ship them. It was a much larger time commitment than I anticipated, and I underestimated the project.

I purchased more tools and increased efforts toward this new hobby. I started to dislike the typewriters and realized I had turned a hobby project into something much more. It started feeling like a business, which was not my intention. Once I became aware of this, I understood my own frustration. The collection was too large and unmanageable as a hobby. I ended up selling and donating many of them and met some incredible fellow enthusiasts along the way. It became fun again, and I have bought a few more rare ones to add to my collection. They have also made great gifts!

Antiques, cars, art, stamps, coins, jewelry, and fine wine are just a few of many collectibles that can appreciate or decline in value over time, much like other investments classified as alternative or tangible assets. Collectors will gather these items because they love them, and an investor will buy them in hopes of appreciation over time with intent to sell at some point. Many collectors are a little of both—they don't intend to sell but like knowing that they could if they wanted to at a profit. Selling collectibles is not always easy and can take time to find the right buyer or reputable auction house to assist. Tax treatment of collectibles is also higher and another consideration to discuss with a tax professional. Other considerations with collectibles are physical protection, insurance protection, and protection against theft.

Nick is a collector with no intention to sell his prized cars, so the only thing he sees is an outflow of money and internal guilt. The sentimental value and enjoyment of the cars are far more important to him than what he could potentially sell them for. Nick can afford to invest in his passion collection because he has overfunded his other goals, but the guilt is taking the joy from something he loves devoting his free time to.

Nick has a great opportunity to share with his son Christopher how he got to where he is financially and why he has the freedom to spend time caring for and building his treasured collection. Christopher may be surprised to learn that there is substantial value in his collection of cars that will likely someday be passed on to him.

Questions to Consider

→ Do you have a hobby, sport, or activity that you feel guilty spending money on?

→ Are you putting money toward this at the expense of your other goals?

→ Are you regularly reviewing your financial plan to ensure you are on track?

Do

➔ Consider establishing a separate account for hobbies, travel, or whatever you want after you have allocated established percentages into the nonnegotiable accounts.

➔ Talk with your partner/spouse about interests/passions/hobbies and write it down so that you are on the same page and in agreement.

➔ Review your financial plan and goals annually and revise if necessary.

Don't

➔ Live in guilt for no reason.

➔ Avoid financial planning because you think you will have to give up things you enjoy.

We all have our own unique interests and things that bring us joy. Some of these things are free, and others can be more costly. This topic isn't about hobbies or interests. Regardless of what your hobby is, it is about how you *feel* about it. Some people spend money they don't have on things they don't necessarily need, and that is a different story. If you are on track to meet your financial goals and are funding the financial nonnegotiables, you have freedom to allocate and spend money on whatever you want—minus the guilt.

9

DILEMMA IN DIVORCE

JAMES SET THE BOX DOWN IN HIS DESIGNATED parking spot at the apartment complex where he lived. The area was now filled with a maze of boxes, some crisp and brand new and others slumped over and sagging from age and the mildew in the basement. It was the annual town-wide yard sale, and he was hoping to make a little extra cash. Ever since his divorce was finalized, he discovered the harsh reality of having to find a job and live on a single income.

"Hey, Dad, ready for me now?" his teenage son, Will, asked as he approached the parking lot.

He hadn't meant for Will to help him with the yard sale. In fact, he wanted to keep it a secret from him. A switch in weekends due to a high school event in the town where Will lived during the week and every other weekend resulted in him staying at James's apartment this weekend versus next. While it was only a thirty-minute drive between his and his ex-wife's condo, he had never planned to live in a different town than his only child. Having always been a persistent presence in the boy's life, James was the parent who showed up at school events and was a regular chaperone on field trips, and his open schedule allowed him to coach Will in soccer, giving him a front-row seat to his son's everyday happenings. And if he could do it all over again, he wouldn't change a thing. His ex-wife, Alice, had a bustling career as an attorney and offered him the space to be the father that his own father was not, filling a void that built on his confidence and transformed who he was at his core.

"If you want to start taking the stuff from that box and lining it up in some fashion on the picnic table, that would be great." James pointed in the direction of the largest box, its flaps open, showcasing a mishmash of sporting gear. He was on the opposite end of the maze, pulling out old cartons of baseball cards and lining them up on a folding table he borrowed from another resident at the complex.

"Catch!" Will wound up and launched a football toward him in a classic game of catch that the two had reverted to whenever it came to big conversations. It was all about engaging in activity while talking, and seldom did they sit across from one another to hold a face-to-face conversation.

The sound of the ball hitting his palm brought back a million memories, most of them made while his ex was working late or away at events with her mounting responsibilities as a partner at the firm. When Will was in first grade, he taught him how to throw and catch a baseball, the methodical steps one takes to oil a glove and hold a bat. In fifth grade, Will requested his presence in the backyard as they kicked a soccer ball back and forth while they plotted ways to convince Alice to get on board with adopting a dog. In sixth grade it was the first crush, and in seventh grade Will confessed about his first broken heart while they tossed this same football to one another.

"Why are you selling all this stuff anyway?" Will paused like he often did to talk, while tossing the ball from palm to palm.

"Because I already have a football for us to use when you're at my place, an autographed one no less." James was well aware of what he was doing. He was trying to divert the question so Will landed in a territory that wouldn't have to touch upon the evils of divorce.

"I don't mean the football, Dad." Will wrapped one giant palm around the ball.

James couldn't help but think about how tiny his hands once were, how there was a time when his chubby little fingers could barely reach around a golf ball. He was officially a teenager, just two months away from his fourteenth birthday.

"I mean all of this." He stretched out his arms and spun in a circle, implying the loop of boxes surrounding him.

"I'm just participating in the town-wide yard sale, that's all." James followed it up with an attempt at humor. "I only want to keep things that spark joy."

Even in his teen years, Will seldom gave his parents grief, but occasionally he would distribute a flippant eye roll. "You sound like Mom."

James wondered if Alice would be doing the same thing if the roles were reversed. If he had continued in his job as a midlevel manager instead of opting to stay home with Will, maybe she would be the one selling off her possessions. He remembered the day he made the decision to leave his well-paid job in corporate America. It was the same day Alice received the news of her promotion to partner. They had been celebrating with a bottle of wine they saved for a special occasion when Alice's excitement started to dull. The reality of the increased workload she'd be taking on hit her hard, and she expressed the guilt she felt for already being so absent from their son's life.

At the time, the idea of James leaving his career temporarily had been a perfect solution to everything. James could be the father he always dreamed of being, and Alice could focus on the career she had desperately wanted since she was in high school. It was a win-win.

People always considered James and Alice a success story. When they got married, they were starting fresh, strapped with student loans and little guidance. They lived in a studio apartment and spent years limiting what they spent their money on. It took some time, but they built their lives up over the years, adding on to the house and paying off debt. They were finally in a place where they could afford the lifestyle they had dreamed of, thanks to Alice's continued growth at her firm. They worked together like a well-oiled machine. Until they didn't.

Alice had always made more than enough money to support the three of them, and her annual bonuses allowed for their savings to grow while also partaking in annual international trips. James never *had* to work, and he surprised himself with how easy being a stay-at-home dad came to him. The guilt of not maintaining his career and financial contribution to the household tugged at him at first, but he quickly adapted to his role at home.

When they decided to divorce, nine years after they got married, they were both in their forties, and the majority of their wealth was tied up in their house and retirement accounts. As a result, they had to sell the house because neither of them could afford to buy the other one out. Alice couldn't afford to refinance and buy him out with the additional alimony and child support expenses, and James didn't have a job yet. The divorce was as amicable as it could be, and they agreed on custody of Will, which relieved some of the stress. However, he still found himself at a loss. He was quickly realizing that the missing time on his résumé would set him back further than he ever imagined. And to make matters worse, his extended medical insurance was on the verge of running out.

"For real, Dad. What's going on?" Will tossed the ball back to him, a silent message to James that he couldn't avoid this conversation no matter how hard he tried.

"I'm unemployable." James felt his shoulders slouch as he looked at his feet. He had always taught Will to be proud of who he was, quirks and all, but here he was, feeling shame in his lack of career.

"Isn't Mom, like, required to support you or something?" Will asked the same question James had been pondering the entire time he and Alice were going through the separation. They stayed together for many years for the sake of Will, and James had assumed that Alice would continue to take care of things until he could get back on his feet.

"Unfortunately, that's not how it works. It's a bit more complicated than that." He tossed the ball back. He was cautious about what he told Will. He didn't want him to think that he regretted giving up a career to raise him. That wouldn't alleviate any of the sadness that Will had already expressed about the situation.

"It's okay; I'll find something." He tossed the ball back. "I have plenty of skills to go around, and luckily a lot of connections I've built up along the way."

The more James thought about it, the more frustrated he grew with his job hunt. Even his friends who owned businesses couldn't find a spot for him because they were all being taken over by new graduates who required less pay. Many of these graduates still lived at home and had yet to face the reality of paying bills. James naively assumed he could just pick up where he left off when he left his midlevel position. At forty-three, he never imagined it would feel so impossible to slide back into his role and move up from there.

Since the divorce, he had been trying to step back into a position that equated to where he was when he left off, but now his alimony was on the verge of running out. Soon, he'd have no medical insurance. It was something he didn't wish upon his own worst enemies. He couldn't afford to live on the same pay the candidates ten years younger than him were accepting in job offers. He had a child, rent to pay by himself, and soon he'd be adding monthly medical insurance to that already daunting list of bills. James had heard horror stories of his friends' divorces, but they all seemed to miraculously recover, so he was still holding onto hope.

What's James's Money Narrative?

When it comes to financial planning, divorce is up there as one of life's biggest challenges. In addition to this major life event being mentally and emotionally exhausting, it is challenging from a financial planning perspective. No one goes into a marriage and builds a divorce into their plan. You can plan for other life-altering events like death and disability with

> No one goes into a marriage and builds a divorce into their plan.

insurance, but unfortunately, there is no such thing as divorce insurance. Even in the most amicable of divorces, it can wreak havoc on the family finances. Suddenly, there is one pot of money and two separate households, two sets of utilities, and two single people paying a higher tax rate than they did as a married couple. Add to this the fact that there are now two separate individuals going after different goals and having to start over.

However, that said, there are some things you can do to be prepared. If there are substantial assets, it is obviously much easier for both parties to move on and start over. If divorce occurs when income is increasing but assets are not, it can be more challenging. As you saw with James's story, when you reenter the workforce after many years, it can be difficult. James's skill set was rusty because he had been out of practice for a long time. While he is *not unemployable*, he may need to broaden the scope of his job search. He may not be able to get exactly what he wants right now, but there is no doubt he needs a paycheck.

I remember placing an ad for an administrative assistant in the late 2000s. We were all recovering from the effects of the recession. I received hundreds of applications for this position and interviewed many in a similar position as James—they had much higher salary requirements and lacked the tech skill set that other applicants with consistent employment had. I empathize with this; it's hard enough to keep up on the ever-changing landscape of technology with consistent efforts. It's a heavy consideration to leave a career, and raising kids full time is a *huge* job. Unfortunately, the spouse who does this tends to get the short end of the stick financially in a divorce.

James faces more challenges now because his priorities have shifted. He became accustomed to caring for his son full time, and now he must reinvent himself while also grieving the end of his marriage. If he and his wife had stayed married, their arrangement of him being the stay-at-home dad while Alice worked would be fine and a win for the family as a whole. He is having a hard time adjusting to the new norm and expectations of him as a single man. And the older we are, the harder this change can be. Unfortunately, age discrimination is a reality, in some industries more than others, and another layer of stress a recent divorcee may encounter.

When James found himself single again, he thought he would have no problem finding a job; he had experience and education in his field and felt he could prove himself if he got a foot in the door. As he started pursuing job opportunities, he felt out of the loop and realized how much had changed in an industry he used to know like the back of his hand.

There are some resources out there for marriage/divorce planning. Prenuptial agreements protect income and assets before a couple gets married, and if there is wealth involved, it can provide protection for a stay-at-home spouse. James and Alice started from scratch and built everything they had together over time, so this type of agreement didn't come into play.

Proactively, I think it is important for couples to have candid conversations regarding money expectations from the start. If James was hesitant to quit his job initially, they may have been able to compromise so he could continue in his field and still play a large part in raising his son versus stepping out completely. Alternately, James and Alice could have established a postnuptial agreement to clearly outline how James would be compensated for giving up his career if the relationship ended in divorce.

First things first. James needs to get a job, and while he may not land in a desired position immediately, he'll have to accept what he can get simply for the paycheck and healthcare benefits. The good news is that James can get back on track fairly quickly if he sets his mind to it. He can sharpen his skill set, but he needs to start somewhere and embrace the challenge.

Questions to Consider

→ Have you had a conversation with your partner or spouse about "what if" scenarios and how they will be handled?

→ Do you have a plan in place for starting a family and potential roles and responsibilities for childcare planning?

→ Do you feel comfortable with the current plan in place?

Do

→ Have frequent household financial conversations with your spouse/ partner.

→ Plan for the best-case scenario but be prepared for other possibilities.

→ Take action and organize your financial picture.

→ Seek professional guidance if necessary.

Don't

→ Assume your partner has everything handled.

→ Ignore warning signs that things may be headed downhill.

I am a proponent of proactive planning, and divorce is no exception. If you feel divorce may be in your future, take action now. Fear can be paralyzing and scary, but preparation is empowering. We should all regularly review our financial picture, and when there are big changes on the horizon, this is top priority. If there are steps that you can start working on to prepare for what is coming, put them in action. This could involve educational development or speaking with an attorney to better understand the process well before any action is necessary.

Let's face it: divorce or the possibility of divorce is not an easy or pleasant thing to think about, let alone prepare for. It might be tempting to ignore it as long as possible, but self-care is one of the only things we can control, and it's especially important when we are going through major life changes and challenges. We've all been presented with ideas for how we can better take care of ourselves. However, we are often directed to yoga, meditation, therapy, etc. Financial organization should be added to that list and is an important component of our overall health.

insufficient funds

10

AN EMPTY BUCKET

HUDSON LOOKED DOWN AT THE ROLEX fastened to his wrist. Five minutes before five. Just in time. He pulled the door open to the restaurant, adjusting his senses to the heightened noise level. It was happy hour at a local restaurant in the financial district, a hangout for the professionals who worked around the clock to gain an edge in a highly competitive industry.

"Over here, Hudson!" A female voice pulled his attention toward a high-top table in the bar area.

He took four long strides until he was front and center with his group of colleagues. "Long time no see." Sarcasm tugged at the edge of his lip, forming a crooked grin.

"I ordered your usual." His team manager, Phoebe, slid a pint across the wobbly table.

"How did you get it so fast?" Hudson inquired, taking pride in the fact that he was never late for anything.

"Oh, I got here a little early for a meeting. Actually, that is one of the reasons why I invited you all out."

Hudson admired Phoebe. The woman had quickly become a legend at their financial firm not long after he started working there eight years ago, and he considered her a mentor.

"So, not all of you will be super excited about this, but I've signed our group up to give presentations at a leadership course the city is hosting next spring."

Hudson felt his eyes grow at the opportunity. Public speaking was something he had mastered over the years, and he'd gotten to the point where he actually enjoyed being on a stage, sharing his financial advice. This wouldn't be the first conference he'd had a chance to serve as a speaker, and if his career climbed the trajectory he'd hoped for, nor would it be the last.

"Count me in." Hudson lifted his glass in a mock cheers.

"So this engagement is a little different from the last," Phoebe started. "It's through an organization whose mission is to share professional tools that can span across all industries."

"So, are we going to be offering advice on building wealth?" a colleague asked.

Phoebe came back quick. "Nope, not this time."

Naturally, Hudson's curiosity was piqued. If he wasn't offering advice about money, then what would he be speaking about?

"The theme of this conference is 'leading by example,' and it will feature speakers from all industries who share examples about how they lead by living what they teach."

Phoebe's words were greeted with positive remarks from most of the colleagues circling the table, but Hudson felt a pang of nerves. Besides reading to his daughter's third-grade class, the only public speaking he did involved finances.

"So, how will that work?" he asked, skepticism hidden beneath the happy curiosity he presented to his boss.

"Well, each one of us will speak about ways our lives have improved by implementing the strategies we help clients within our own lives." Phoebe sliced her hands through the air as she spoke, spurring the same intensity that she had when she spoke about budgeting and retirement planning. "For example, Hudson, you might want to talk about the ways that you incorporate financial organization in your own life."

Hudson was well versed in the bucket system. After all, he'd been advising his clients for years on putting plans in place for spending and investing. Just earlier today he was guiding a middle-aged couple about how they could save more money. Voicing their concern over the impending college debt that was looming over their heads as their two children neared the end of high school, they came to him for advice on how they could step up their savings without having to forego the family fun they'd always looked forward to. As if he had memorized a script, Hudson had rattled off all the ways they could implement the bucket system with the same intensity that Phoebe was using right now.

"Oh, this could be fun," another colleague interjected. Normally Hudson would've been on board with the excitement, but there was something that was bothering him, and he couldn't figure out what it was.

"So, Hudson, you love to speak. Let's get right to it, and this will be a piece of cake come springtime." Phoebe passed him the reassuring smile she always gave him when he was learning something new. It had always comforted him in the past, but he was struggling to feel a sense of relief. "How have the financial strategies you help your clients with changed your life?"

The pitch of the voices and laughter at the nearby tables seemed to rise, sending a shock of nerves through Hudson as he tried to think of an answer. The eyes of his colleagues stared at him, awaiting a response that he didn't have. "Um … well … I—"

Time stood still until he was saved by another colleague who shared the details about how her family decides on a fun activity to do together, based on the amount of money they've allotted in their entertainment fund.

"Sometimes we order from our favorite pizza place, or sometimes we'll save up more and go away for a night. The kids love that it gives them something to look forward to, and we are teaching them about how to budget without having to scream it in their faces."

The circle of colleagues chimed in with all-knowing chuckles, but Hudson wasn't laughing on the inside.

When the conversation transpired into each of the colleagues' stories about leading by example, Hudson's face flushed. Instead of contributing to the discussion, he found himself feeling like an outsider. All this time, as his clients' money was snowballing, his money was running thin. Instead of following his own advice, like his colleagues were doing, he spent more money than he had. The more he listened to them discussing their commitment and success in their personal lives, the more Hudson started to perspire as he thought about his own financial situation.

Instead, he was wrapped in the harsh reality that he hadn't lived by his own principles. He knew all the right questions to ask and had taken every professional development course offered to him, continuously on a mission to attain many well-deserved acronyms after his name. Instead of incorporating all the knowledge he acquired in the industry through education and experience, Hudson instead let his own finances ride an untethered wave.

He hadn't set his own family's financial future up for success. The weight of this realization paired with the idea that every one of his colleagues seemed to have their financial affairs in order and their big picture plans on the right track concealed who he always thought he was with a layer of insecurity. He had never consulted with anyone about his personal planning for unbiased feedback.

On the outside he expressed joy for his clients' success and dedication, but on the inside he was filled with a sobering shame. While he told his clients to pay off debt, he had been accumulating it, making purchases that were beyond his family's means to maintain an image he felt he needed. As he reiterated the importance of an emergency fund to others, he fell short with his own.

Hudson's mind started racing about this sudden burst of internal honesty. His oldest was approaching the college application stage of high school, but he didn't have a college fund for either of the kids. He encouraged discipline to invest at least 15 percent of income toward investments but made excuses and fell short with his own plan. Hudson stressed the importance of adequate insurance for his clients but still hadn't taken out a life insurance policy for himself or his wife, who had been a stay-at-home mom for the past fifteen years.

Hudson's silence during this conversation didn't go unnoticed on Phoebe, and after their coworkers dispersed, she asked Hudson to stay for another round.

"So, what's up?" she started. "I'm sensing apprehension about this team event. I thought you were our keynote speaker," she said with a smile.

Hudson couldn't keep quiet any longer. "I guess I feel like I might not be the right person to give this speech." He toyed with the edge of the paper napkin with sweaty fingertips.

Phoebe let out a loud one-syllable laugh. "Ha! You always seem so calm while you're speaking in front of a crowd."

"It's not that. It's just that I haven't really been leading by example." Before he could stop himself, his nerves led the parade of confessions that spilled out of his mouth. "I have credit card debt that has gotten out of hand, I am underfunded for retirement and the kids' college, and I don't even have an adequate emergency fund." He paused, realizing the napkin was now shredded. He wiped the tiny paper particles onto his still perfectly pressed black pants.

"And the worst part is that my wife thinks I have everything in good order. And why wouldn't she? I'm an advisor, and this is what I do day in and day out, but I can't seem to get my own family's affairs in order. I'm literally immersed in this stuff all day, but I've been avoiding my own financial picture and making excuses, which is exactly what I tell other people not to do."

Phoebe's next words came out the same way they did when she was teaching her staff a new tool. "It's not impossible," she said, unfazed by his confessions.

"Hudson, you're not the first person I have worked with who has failed to apply the base principles of our business to his or her own life. It happens in this industry and others. Luckily you are still fairly young in your career, and you are ready to change it; you can turn this around quickly, and you will be so happy you did."

What's Hudson's Money Narrative?

Hudson's story is quite common and spans across different industries. Cobbler's children syndrome is coined after an old proverb about the children of shoemakers who have no shoes. It is more common with entrepreneurs who are so busy helping others that they do not help themselves.

True passion is contagious, and when we follow what brings us joy, we naturally inspire others, which sets a rippling effect in motion. We all veer away from our authentic selves from time to time, and that's okay. We are human, and personal growth is a never-ending journey.

Hudson is methodically helping others, but he isn't helping himself, which is hurting him more than anyone else because he is missing out on being part of the process. Hudson has the luxury of daily immersion in financial matters by being "in the game" every day but is blocking his own financial picture versus embracing it.

Hudson has an opportunity to dramatically improve his personal and professional life by shifting this. His client relationships will be stronger if he is applying the principles he teaches in his own life, and he will be happier and more confident as a result.

Hudson needs to come clean with his wife and lay out the reality of their financial picture. She has a right to know the truth about their numbers and may understandably be upset; she trusts him not only as her partner but also as someone who works in a field with high ethical standards. I can't speak to what will result from the conversation, but if we assume that Hudson and his wife are able to work through this, their next steps should be taken together.

Hudson and his wife should consider "hiring" another advisor, possibly Phoebe, to analyze their financial picture and help them create their own plan and action steps. Together, they can tackle the debt, emergency fund, and insurance gaps first. Hudson will benefit from the accountability to his wife, and Phoebe will be more likely to help them put their plan into action. Sometimes, we have blinders on when looking at our own lives, and the lens unintentionally changes. It may seem odd for a planner to hire a planner, but it's a valuable testament to our integrity in what we do for our clients and the integrity of the business as a whole. It is also valuable to go through the process of planning on the other side of the table.

Before I started as a financial planner, I left a career in the mortgage business, which felt "reactive" at the time. In the mid-2000s and up until the Great Recession of 2008, many used their houses as a constant source of additional cash to buy things they didn't need and couldn't afford. Armed with my past experience, I entered this business hopeful to flip the switch to a proactive approach that would thrive with the presence of a plan to apply in my own life along with my future clients.

Starting out as a financial advisor, I felt overwhelmed. While I had passed all the required tests for entry, there was nothing that could have prepared me for the massive amount of industry knowledge that I would need to acquire to stay afloat as an advisor. In the early days, I leaned heavily on others for support, and after a decade I'm still learning new things every day in this business. I feel fortunate to be in a position where I can celebrate my clients' successes when they see positive improvements, and I feel privileged that they trust me to be the one to walk alongside them. I've spent thousands of hours with clients and prospective clients sharing their stories, and I always try to put myself in their shoes. There are many situations I can relate to and others that I empathize with. In turn, this naturally led me to constantly self-analyze my own financial picture. In the first few years, I put many strategies in place for myself as I did for my clients. My clients help me just as much as I help them, and that is a priceless bonus working in this field.

Financial planning is for everyone, not just the wealthy. Creating simple documents such as a will, medical directives, and a password organizer provides peace of mind in the present and for our loved ones in the future. Once the fundamentals are in place, additional gaps can be filled as circumstances and needs change.

Hudson has taken an admirable first step by acknowledging the problem and has the added benefit of already knowing what he needs to do. With some accountability and discipline, he can turn his situation around quickly.

Questions to Consider

➜ Are there gaps in your financial plan or with those who are close to you (i.e., parents)?

➜ Are you setting aside time regularly to review your own goals and tracking your progress?

➜ Are there topics you are avoiding because they are too confusing or stressful to think about?

Do

➜ Start a conversation with your partner/spouse or loved ones and ask questions. If they do not want to engage, at least you tried.

➜ Think about your top three financial concerns right now and write down actions you can take this week to gather more information and take action.

➜ Consider getting a second opinion and adding professional help to your household financial team.

Don't

➜ Avoid addressing topics that are keeping you up at night. It may be easier than you think to explore solutions and positive changes.

Financial planning is unique for everyone, and it is heavily dependent on what stage of life you're in and your habits and discipline levels. For instance, there are some people who can have a credit card that they religiously pay off every month, racking up points as they go along. And there are others who need to hide their credit card until they build better habits. Financial planning is not a one-size-fits-all process. There are fundamentals that we all need to have in place, which include an emergency fund, proper insurance coverages and invest-ment vehicles, and an estate plan.

If there are big gaps in between where you are and where you want to be, bigger shifts and new habits may be necessary. In the end, it's incredibly rewarding to have a plan in place and the peace of mind that comes along with it knowing your finances are in good order, with all the foundational nonnego-tiables accounted for. Financial stress is fairly common, but it usually stems from allowing money to control us and worries that we allow to snowball over time. Planning is dynamic, and none of us can predict the future. We can't control what happens in our country on a national or global scale, but we can control our finances and dramatically increase our odds of success.

11

THE UNEXPECTED WIDOW

SOPHIA STOOD FROZEN IN FRONT OF THE COLLECTION of photos that hung on her living room wall. A mishmash of memories dating back to the first date she had with Ben and extending outward to moments that marked their thirty years together. A photo of when their youngest son was born, with his big brother peeking over Sophia's shoulder, one of the family gathered around a new puppy they'd surprised the kids with at Christmas, the quintessential cap and gown photo taken the day their oldest son graduated from college. And then, front and center, was the photo of her and her late husband, Ben, their heads tipped back in laughter as they sat on a picnic blanket.

Even after all those years, she still remembered how she had already been smitten with him on that first date. Taking the picture was her best friend, who had been picnicking with her now husband. It was the double date that would kick off many double dates for years to come. Except Sophia would now be the third wheel. She pulled the frame off the wall and ran a finger along the glass, hoping to somehow turn back time and free her from the grief she was experiencing at the unexpected loss of her beloved husband.

With delicate movements, she set the frame on the rolltop desk that sat beneath the photo wall and slowly eased into the chair, sending one loud creak through the quiet space. It was the same sound she heard when she received the news of Ben's passing. She had dropped into this chair when Ben's colleague and best friend called, his voice hidden behind tears.

"Ben had a sudden heart attack. I'm so sorry. He was so healthy. I don't know what happened." The two had worked together at the electrical company for thirty years.

And they still didn't know what happened, no matter how many questions Sophia asked herself and his doctor. He had zero signs of someone who was struggling with heart disease, and it didn't run in his family. She knew this because just months before they were at a family gathering and they were discussing hereditary health conditions. Cancer was a concern in his family, not heart disease. He was only sixty-one years old.

The night before Sophia received the worst news of her life, she and Ben had been bowling at the local lanes where they partook in a weekly game with friends. Ben was his normal competitive self, cracking jokes against the other players and putting forth his best footwork on the lanes and even getting three strikes in a row for the first time. He played a good game, and now he was gone, without so much as a subtle warning. The call felt like a joke, a cruel one, and now she was still trying to sort out her thoughts.

What was she going to do with her life now? Would the pain of grief ever go away?

And then there was the sting that came when she thought about how Ben had gotten to a point in his career where he had achieved the service years required to max out his pension when he retired. This was a goal he had talked about their entire marriage, and now, just like that, he would never be able to enjoy it.

Sophia herself had never worked much besides a part-time job here and there, but she always admired her husband's dedication to his company.

The creak of the chair, like everything else in the house, sparked another memory. This was Ben's desk, the place where he paid the bills, did his crossword puzzles, and read the daily newspaper. The creaky chair had been a point of contention for them up until the very moment his heart attack stole his life. Just days before, she had been telling him to tighten the screws in the chair, a reminder that had started as subtle and developed into an annoyance over the months.

The desk, with the top rolled up, was neatly organized with new checkbooks, envelopes, and a stack of crossword puzzles Ben didn't have a chance to finish. Sophia pulled in a long, slow breath, hoping to escape the anxiety that was brewing within, as she looked around at the foreign space. Ben had handled the bills for as long as she could remember. And now, with the funeral behind her, she was tasked with sorting through the bills and figuring out what needed to be paid and when. She'd been so absent from this part of their relationship for so long that she felt completely lost, as if she was learning another language. The first checkbook in the stack was crisp, just ready to be used, but she had no clue what was due to be paid. When her search in the drawers beneath the desk led to no clear answers, she felt helpless and was overcome with yet another bout of tears—this time they were salty droplets of frustration.

$ $ $

Since they started dating, Sophia and Ben had been together more hours than not, and they had always been attentive to communicating with one another, except when it came to finances. This had always been an area that Ben took over and enjoyed. It worked out well considering financial topics overwhelmed her. The blend of confusion and grief was quickly smothered by a feeling of guilt. Why hadn't she asked him more questions? He had always tried to keep her in the loop by talking to her about their accounts, but she shut him down, afraid that her feeling of being overwhelmed would take over, so he stopped trying.

What accounts did they have and how would she be able to access them?

While Ben wasn't known for his tech savviness, there were several bills that likely had to be paid online, which meant that she had another barrier standing in her way: passwords. She had scoured every drawer, and not a single password list came to fruition. As tears cascaded down her cheeks, she pressed the keyboard on the wobbly desk and attempted to try a variety of different letter and number combinations to get into Ben's computer.

What's Sophia's Money Narrative?

My heart goes out to Sophia and the weight of grief she is going through from losing her husband. She is dealing with so many emotions simultaneously and is likely running on minimal capacity to deal with the financial parts of the picture.

Prior to my becoming a financial planner, my father passed away unexpectedly. During the months that followed, my family and I experienced heightened stress stacked on top of grief when we discovered the many financial pieces that were in disarray. My mom wasn't prepared to deal with the financial aspects on top of the sudden loss of her husband. She had never been involved in any part of the household finances, and it worked for them, until my dad was no longer around to do it. In the months that followed, my siblings and I worked through the gaps and pieced together their financial puzzle.

I wholeheartedly believe that my dad would have planned differently had he known what was coming. His family was everything to him, and he wanted harmony among all of us. The problem is life is unpredictable, and sometimes our time here is cut short unexpectedly. Procrastination can come with a hefty penalty when it comes to certain aspects of planning.

> My personal experience with my dad's passing sparked my interest in learning as much as I could about financial planning, which evolved into a passion for helping others do the same.

My personal experience with my dad's passing sparked my interest in learning as much as I could about financial planning, which evolved into a passion for helping others do the same. I have worked with many widows and widowers over the years, and all handle grief in different ways. Sometimes, it can be therapeutic to gain control over what you can when everything feels out of control, and financial security is often at the top of the list. Sophia is overwhelmed and may be questioning if she is going to be okay.

Hopefully, Sophia's name is on the bank accounts so that she can access statements and records and continue to pay the monthly bills. If not, she will likely need to hire an estate attorney for assistance to gain access. Nowadays, most statements are paperless, which can make this process more challenging.

There are a few things Sophia can do to get organized. If possible, she should ask a trusted friend or responsible child for help locating important documents and creating a to-do list.

First things first, she should contact the family CPA or tax professional to identify interest/dividends paid. The CPA will likely have all the tax documents from the previous years, which will identify the account numbers and location of where they are held. This will be the best way to find online accounts that she may not be aware of. She will need to call the banks and investment companies to let them know her husband has passed away. Hopefully, her husband has her listed as a beneficiary on any retirement accounts. If not, she will need legal guidance to sort through the next steps.

Ben's employer will be able to assist her with any life insurance that he has through employment, and additional life insurance contracts should be accessible in their financial files. She should also ask the bank if there are any safe-deposit boxes that are registered in his name because people often store important documents there if they have one.

Hopefully, Sophia will be able to gain access to the computer to check the history and see if there are any additional logins that she should look into for potential accounts and assets. She will be able to piece through this over time and reregister accounts and get things in good order, but it will likely cause additional stress for her during a very difficult time.

It is very common for one spouse to handle the majority of household financial matters—especially in the silent generation, born between 1925 and 1945, and the Baby Boomer generation, born between 1946 and 1964.

If financial planning discussions are not your cup of tea, that is fine, but I think it is a good idea to at least know what you have as a couple and where things are. An overview or snapshot of your financial household picture can save a lot of heartache down the road. I have worked with many where only one partner wants to engage in review meetings, but when we are doing a financial plan or initial review, I encourage everyone to come to the table for this reason.

It is important to regularly check beneficiary designations to ensure that they are up to date. Marriage does not take precedence over what is written down on a beneficiary document; financial institutions will only pay out to the designated beneficiary. If no beneficiary is listed, it will go to probate, and this takes time and is very easy to avoid by regularly reviewing this information.

Sophia's situation has additional challenges; however, she will be able to get on track over time. Proactively, this can be avoided with basic steps and planning.

Online organization can be efficient and convenient for document storage and management, but I recommend a binder with paper copies of important information, including:

- Contact information for your CPA, estate-planning attorney, financial advisor, and insurance agents

- Account numbers and contact information for all utilities, fixed household expenses, and debts (mortgage, cars, etc.)

- Account registrations and beneficiary information

- Computer access passwords

- A list of all insurance coverages and contact information (auto, home, and umbrella policies)

- A copy of estate-planning documents (wills, trusts, medical directives)

- A copy of year-end statements for all bank and investment accounts to be updated each year

- A copy of your most recent tax return

- A copy of your most recent financial plan

- Any other important access information (safe-deposit boxes, vault codes, etc.)

- Information/pictures of valuables and collectibles that others likely wouldn't know; household inventory is also important for insurance purposes, and a copy should also be added to your online storage account if you have one (i.e., Dropbox or Box)

- A list of subscriptions, memberships, and other ongoing payments that should be canceled when a spouse passes; this could include health club memberships, professional associations, magazine subscriptions, etc.

Questions to Consider

→ Are you and your partner/spouse prepared if something unexpected happened to one of you?

→ Are you regularly reviewing your financial and estate plan to ensure all is up to date?

→ Do you need to create a new plan of action if financial and estate plans are not in place?

Do

→ Have a conversation with your partner/spouse and make sure you are both "in the know" with your household expenses and financial accounts.

→ Put together a financial organization binder and review together.

→ Make this a priority and seek professional guidance if necessary.

Don't

→ Assume that your partner knows how to manage things without conversation and review.

→ Avoid it and figure you can address it "down the road."

→ Be afraid of the process because you don't want to think about it; organization will give you both peace of mind and can be a good project to work through together.

The thought of losing a loved one or the idea of our own death can understandably be a topic we prefer to avoid. As Benjamin Franklin famously said, "Nothing is certain, except death and taxes."[2] In addition to you and your partner/spouse knowing the location of the binder, share the location with

---

2   Christopher Bullock, *The Cobbler of Preston*, 1716.

an additional trusted friend or family member. The binder may take a few hours to organize, but the benefits will be rewarding—peace of mind in the present and a priceless gift to leave behind for your loved ones.

12

LIFE-CHANGING WINDFALL

SADIE HAD BEEN WORKING AS DYLAN'S EXECUTIVE
assistant for six years, but she still got nervous when
she was called into his office. Working for a Silicon
Valley start-up was certainly exciting; however, strategies and
plans changed often, and there were a lot of ups and downs.
It was nearing the end of the year, a time when Dylan had a
tendency to get hyped up about future goal setting. If the past
was any inclination, he would likely be requesting her list of
personal and professional goals for the new year. Knowing
that her boss was determined to make his staff as goal oriented

as he was, Sadie came with her list prepared and had her tablet on and ready to take notes. She sipped in a breath of air as she knocked just beneath the sign that read Dylan O'Neil, CEO. Beneath that was the company logo.

She took one last look around the office, the empty space a confirmation that the holidays were here and that the majority of her colleagues were taking their remaining vacation days to spend time with their families. As always, with the exception of Kyle, Sadie had been the last one to leave the office before the doors closed for Christmas Eve. That ongoing inkling of doubt crept up her spine one last time as she stood outside her boss's door. *Would this be the time he fired her? Let her go for a younger assistant who was more tech savvy and required less pay?*

As always, Dylan greeted her at the door. Unlike bosses she had previously in her career as an executive assistant, Dylan treated her like an equal. And the smile on his face as he swung the door open and ushered her into his spacious office gave her a smidge of hope that she wasn't being called in for termination.

"Take a seat." He stood behind a large table that he used as a desk, made even bigger because there were few items on it. Dylan was proud of his minimalist approach to work and life and often discussed its relation to success and happiness. He joined Sadie and dropped into a gray chair on the other side of his desk. Behind him, a single white shelf hung on the wall with three Malcolm Gladwell hardcover books with the spines facing outward, their titles perfectly aligned.

"So, are you ready for the holidays?"

It was a question that may be a vehicle for finding out if Sadie finally had a boyfriend. But the answer was always the same. At forty-three years old, she had yet to meet someone who was worth the time, and besides, she was happy with the small group of friends she spent Christmas and New Year's with.

"Yep, just a few more items to wrap for the annual gift exchange tonight, but other than that, I'm ready." She fiddled with the zipper on her backpack. "And you?"

"Oh, yeah … this year I'm heading up north for a ski trip. A little getaway." A smile tugged at the edge of his lips, and that's when Sadie realized something was off with her boss. He never went away or left the vicinity of the company, in case something needed his immediate attention. And something *always* needed his attention.

Sadie tilted her head to the side and passed him a curious look. "You're going away?"

"Actually, yes, that's the reason why I called you down here." Dylan smoothed a hand on the desk and analyzed his palm as if he was looking for a speck of dust that wasn't there. His hand was free of a wedding ring and would likely remain that way as long as he was attached to his career and the business he built from the ground up. The company had quickly become the go-to for business coaches everywhere. The user-friendly tracking system allowed both the client and the coach to interact seamlessly.

While Sadie was by no means high on the totem pole of the company, she was his right hand and often tended to tasks that were above her $60,000 salary. "What can I do while you're away?" She jumped right in, ready to take on a few extra responsibilities.

"Nothing." Dylan leaned forward and steepled his hands together. "So I want to share some news that could potentially impact you in a significant way."

Oh great, Sadie thought. *He's giving me bad news right before Christmas, so I can recover over the break.* "Okay." She maintained her composure and braced herself for his next words.

"I've engaged an investment banker to work with the company on an IPO filing. The board of directors has signed off. If all goes according to plan, we will become a public company next year. I'm letting you know before others in the company because I will need your help as we make plans."

If Sadie wasn't frozen by the news, she would've fallen back in her chair from the shock of her boss's announcement. A million questions stormed through her mind at once. The first among them was, *What does this mean for me?*

"Wow. That was not what I was expecting you to say." Sadie didn't have to say too much more. Her face had already contorted into a series of expressions that showed surprise, confusion, and then surprise again.

"I was hopeful we would eventually go public. Our investors and employees like you have sacrificed a lot for the company." He leaned back in his chair, rocking gently. "Sadie, you've been with me for a while, and we've always known that your salary is a little on the low side. However, you've been accumulating stock options in yearly grants. We won't know until sometime in the middle of next year if we can even do a successful IPO. There are no guarantees. However, if the market for companies like ours remains strong, your options will likely be worth somewhere in the low sevens. You'll be a millionaire. I would recommend that you find a good financial planner right away. And we need to keep this quiet for now until we're a little further along in the process and I can tell the entire company."

What's Sadie's Money Narrative?

Silicon Valley is a hub for technology innovation and entrepreneurial spirit. There are countless start-ups with the goal of acquisition or going public, and they sometimes result in financial windfalls for those involved.

Sadie is in a great position, and her dedication to Dylan and the company may pay off in a big way, assuming that all goes smoothly from this point to the IPO date.

When the news eventually is released to the rest of the company, the excitement and buzz in the office will be contagious. This is what all start-ups are striving toward; however, very few make it to this point. Sadie will likely be part of endless conversations with fellow colleagues calculating their near future wealth. There will be advice and strategy conversations entertained, and financial advisors will be ready and waiting to assist.

$ $ $

Sadie's confusion and excitement are understandable. Even though this has been the goal for the company all along, they were all aware of the odds they faced. The good news is that Sadie has time to sort through her choices because it will be months before she will be able to act on any decisions.

Many start-ups issue incentive stock options (ISOs) as part of employee compensation packages. An employee is granted a specific number of options with the right but not the obligation to purchase stock in the future at a fixed price. As options vest, they can be exercised by the employee if they choose, or they can wait to exercise options.

Typically, an employee has a fixed number of years (often ten) to exercise options after they vest, and if they don't, the options become worthless, so it is a good idea to know the details. Often there are provisions, such as if they leave the company or if there is a change of control such as the company is acquired, and the window can dramatically shorten.

It is highly advisable for Sadie to seek professional guidance with the next steps; all is not easy street from here. The tax treatment varies based on the type of options she holds, and strategy around exercising and selling can be complex. If you aren't an expert or don't have a financial professional with an expertise in IPOs and ISOs on your team, a financial hardship could be mistakenly triggered, resulting in unintended consequences such as an unexpected heavy tax burden or large cash outlay.

For this story, we will assume all goes as planned and Sadie's net worth has increased dramatically. At this point, she is likely very attached to her company's success, and it may be tempting to hold all of this stock with the assumption that continued growth is inevitable. Since she has the majority of her net worth and paycheck all coming from the same company, she should strongly consider a systematic plan to sell shares and diversify into other investments over time to reduce her concentration risk, with guidance on strategy from her financial and tax advisors.

Sadie's story may not feel relatable for those who have never worked in the tech/start-up space, but the general guidance would apply to other situations as well. Many people have a significant part of their wealth tied up in one asset—perhaps they own a family business or inherited a large vacation home. When I worked in the mortgage business, there were many who had the majority of their net worth tied up in real estate holdings, and the 2008 recession caught many off guard, resulting in overleveraged positions that were underwater.

In lending, I noticed that banks are more than willing to lend when you don't need the money, but the minute you do, it's a different story. In 2007, I had an open line of credit, and I received a letter from the bank stating the credit line was being reduced from $150,000 to $1,000 with no warning or reasoning. As panic set in, banks began to pull back credit lines and tighten the purse strings. At the time, I saw that as an emergency source of funds if needed and learned quickly that

I was not viewing this the right way; there is a big difference between an emergency fund that I own versus an emergency fund that belongs to the bank.

$ $ $

Diversification will help Sadie manage her overall risk by investing her assets into different companies, industries, and asset classes versus one single company. My suggestion is to do this strategically with a set schedule rather than obsessively watch the market and attempt to choose an ideal time. She will likely always have additional unvested stock, so there will be opportunity on the horizon if things go up while protecting herself and her assets if values go down.

Very few start-ups make it to this point, which puts Sadie in an incredible and enviable position. With commitment and a solid financial team, she can create a winning plan and set herself up for continued success and future opportunities.

Questions to Consider

→ Are your investments diversified?

→ Do you have a single concentrated position in one sector or industry that you need to address?

→ Has an outside professional reviewed your strategy for feedback?

Do

→ Review your investment and asset allocation regularly and rebalance as necessary.

→ Take the emotion/attachment out of highly concentrated positions and focus on your short- and long-term goals.

→ Seek professional guidance for a second opinion on your strategy.

Don't

→ Ignore company benefits such as stock, especially if it is a large percentage of your net worth.

→ Allow concentrated risk to grow and ignore reviewing your strategy.

→ Be afraid to ask questions; contact your HR department for clarification on any language in your contract that is unclear or confusing.

Whether you work for a start-up, a publicly traded company, or a nonpublicly traded company or you are a business owner, diversification is an important component of your investment plan. As certain asset classes grow or decrease more than others, you may become overweighted or underweighted over time. Periodic reviews are a critical part of portfolio maintenance and necessary to address unsystematic risks that can be managed. Investing carries systematic/market risk that is generally unavoidable, but investing through multiple vehicles, industries, and companies can mitigate risk in your overall strategy.

OUR
BUSINESS

13

THE FAMILY BUSINESS

KEITH SWUNG THE DOOR OPEN TO THE HIBACHI restaurant. The familiar scent of spices and sizzling meats hit his nose as soon as he stepped inside. The spot was where Barrett Plumbing employees met every time there was something to celebrate. Tonight he had something big to tell his employees. He scanned the dining room until his gaze landed on the company's go-to table. A small round one that normally sat five, but like every other dinner meeting with management, there would only be three diners: Keith; his son Brandon; and his daughter, Amelia. He smiled like he always did when he saw his two children and then made a beeline for the table.

"I'm starving." There was no need for a formal greeting.

"Did you ever manage to get off the phone with Mrs. Rockwell?" Brandon asked, as he sipped his water.

"Yes, finally. That's why I'm a tad late." He looked down at his phone and saw that he was fifteen minutes late. He called the meeting earlier this morning, but as always with any business, there was really no closing time. They had hours of operation, but plumbing issues arose at all hours of the day and night, and someone had to be there to handle the customers.

"Well, don't be mad, but we may have started without you." Amelia smiled as she pushed a plate of appetizers in Keith's direction.

"I expect nothing less," Keith said as he plucked a skewer of meat from the plate. "Thanks for coming tonight."

Amelia and Brandon responded with raised brows, questioning the rare show of gratitude. He knew that he was rough around the edges, and he even surprised himself by the acknowledgment of thanks. If he was being honest with himself, he was excited and nervous all at the same time.

"So I called this meeting for a reason."

Brandon and Amelia exchanged confused glances as their father continued.

"You both have already taken over a lot of the business responsibilities, and I think you're both more than capable of taking it over from here."

"Taking it over?" Brandon turned toward Keith.

"Yes … I'm ready to retire." The words came out even more matter-of-factly than he planned.

"You are going to completely step down?" Amelia leaned back in her chair as if she just got hit by a big gust of wind. He wasn't surprised by that, considering he always thought he'd work until he could no longer walk. But slowly, the idea of retirement started tugging at him as he watched his friends one by one punch out for the last time.

"Yes." It was a simple answer, yet he could see the lineup of questions that Brandon and Amelia still had, and he let them fire away.

"How exactly will that work?" Brandon started. "We don't have the money to buy you out."

"I'm not looking for a lump sum. Just give me a monthly amount for life and take care of Mom if and when anything happens to me."

"What about Mark?" Amelia interjected. Her other brother had always mentioned that he wanted to come back to the business at some point.

Keith waved her off. "You can deal with that when the time comes."

"Well, how will the other employees deal with this change?"

"Oh, they will be just fine. They know us ... we're family. It's not like I'm handing it over to a stranger who is going to come in and make all these changes," Keith said matter-of-factly.

What's Keith's Money Narrative?

Family businesses have unique characteristics when compared to other businesses. The close tie between parents and their children and their partners creates a special dynamic.

My dad owned a trucking company, and all of my siblings and I worked in the business in one capacity or another over the years. Starting when I was twelve, I did the billing for the company, which was a task that was passed on to me from my older brother. I also manned the phones and did dispatch during summer months; back then we used walkie talkies, and as a kid, it was fun to use radio language and say things like "10-4." I was always happy to make the extra money, and I learned a lot at a young age about invoicing and accounts receivable (and the stress that goes along with waiting for them). Two of my older brothers went on to take over the business, and the rest of us did other things.

$ $ $

Keith may be ready to retire, or maybe he feels that it is time to give the kids full control over the business. These are his children, and he trusts them, so he is approaching the next steps in a casual way. There are a few things that should be considered as he plans the next steps.

Ideally, succession planning is started far in advance for any business to properly prepare all parties involved for the transition. In this case, the kids may know how to run the business for the most part, but there are likely many things that Keith hasn't passed over and long-term clients involved, which could impact business retention and growth.

Despite the significant trust involved, writing things down and having an open conversation about all potential outcomes are important. What happens if revenue decreases? Does the stipend amount change too? How will it be handled if one of the siblings decides to leave and pursue another venture? What if the third sibling comes into the picture years from now and wants ownership too? Is this business legally owned by the two siblings only? What if Keith passes away, and the mother decides to remarry and her income increases?

> Ideally, succession planning is started far in advance for any business to properly prepare all parties involved for the transition.

And does Keith know if the kids actually want to take over the business? He worked so hard to build the business into what it is that he may be assuming the kids will consider this a great gift, but they may not see it that way.

One of the problems with a verbal agreement with multiple people involved is that the various parties in the conversation may remember the details differently, and there may be no ill intention involved. However, with something as large as running a business, this can cause even bigger problems.

Keith's intentions are good, and his heart is in the right place. He seems to be treating this situation similar to how he treated other situations involving his children—with the trust and comfort he's established with them over the years. Handing over the business is likely stemmed in generous intention and may work out in the long run; however, by addressing some of these questions and making the transition and terms crystal clear, he will add a layer of comfort for all parties involved. This will give his kids a winning start and greater chance of successfully carrying on what he worked so hard to build.

Keith should consider buy/sell insurance policies in lieu of a lump sum buyout, which will be paid by the business with him and his wife as the beneficiaries. If something happens to either one of them, the death benefit could pay off the stipend in full to either parent and serve as the source of additional income they need in retirement.

Keith could also stay on in a part-time role so that he is still involved for a while. This will also allow him to meet with clients as they transition for retention and overall comfort. It will also be reassuring for the other employees and any apprehension they may have with the transition.

Questions to Consider

→ Do you have a death/disability plan in place? (If you died or became disabled today due to an unforeseen tragedy and are unable to run the business, who will step in?)

→ Have you thought about a succession plan and how you see the business transferring when you choose to retire (i.e., a key employee taking it over and purchasing, working with a business broker, or hiring for the purpose of succession)?

➤ If you are running a family business, have you talked with your kids about whether they want to purchase and take over the business someday? If you plan to gift the business, will this create any financial hardship for you in retirement?

Do

➤ Proactive business planning yearly and include death/disability and succession planning in the long-term picture.

➤ Have conversations with family members who work for you if you are considering them as your potential succession plan to ensure everyone is on the same page.

➤ Research and hire help if you need it; there are professionals who are trained in this, and many specialize in specific industries.

➤ Once you have a succession plan in place, prepare legal documentation or agreements to ensure your wishes and avoid potential conflict.

Don't

➤ Handle business arrangements with family differently than you would with anyone else. A written plan protects everyone involved and minimizes potential conflict.

➤ Avoid it. The further you are away from exiting a business, the more you can plan for a successful eventual transition.

Family businesses and small businesses are more likely to ignore succession planning. It may be because they do not have someone to sell the business to, they plan to work forever, or they think there is no significant value attached to the business. We don't always have control over when we exit, and it is important to protect what you have worked hard to build. The value of a robust small business can turn into a nice stream of income in retirement if a plan is in place.

Additionally, when hiring others who are solo practitioners and a part of your financial team, ask them what their succession plan is. There are many CPAs, financial advisors, and attorneys who operate as solo practitioners. There is nothing wrong with this, but it is important for you to know what happens if something unforeseen happens to them. For instance, who will step in to manage things in the process, or what will happen to important hardcopy documents, etc.?

14

A TALE OF TWO SISTERS

ELLA'S HAND TREMBLED AS SHE SWIPED AN INDEX finger across the screen of her phone. As someone who despised conflict, she was dreading the call she had to make to her twin sister, Charlotte. She could no longer sit back and watch her sister blow away the inheritance money their beloved grandfather left them.

"Hello, sister," Charlotte said through sips of air. "Sorry, I just finished teaching a class. Evidently, at forty-one, I'm not in the same shape that I was in as a kid."

Her laughter punched the earpiece and sent a ripple of bittersweet emotions through Ella. She loved hearing her sister's voice and was grateful Charlotte was still immersed in the dance world that she cherished, but she was angry with her financial irresponsibility.

"Hi, Char … listen; I have something to tell you."

Knowing her sister, Ella knew it would be best to dive right in, before Charlotte got on to another topic. The two looked identical, still even in their forties, but they were the proud owners of very different personalities. Charlotte's conversational style was jumpy with limited attention to one topic, while Ella could dive into one discussion for hours.

"Uh oh, let me guess … you're calling to lecture me on my spending habits."

"Char, listen, lecturing you is the last thing I want to do, but I'm worried about you. Since Pops died, you've been spending money on—"

"Don't you want me to be happy, Ella?" Charlotte retorted. "Pops left us that money to enjoy ourselves."

Ella remembered what the financial planner had said during their first meeting. "No, actually he left it so we would be comfortable in retirement or use it toward a life goal. Last I checked, a new Mercedes and an all-expenses paid vacation for you and four of your girlfriends wasn't exactly what he had in mind for a life goal."

"And how do you know what his idea of a life goal was?" Charlotte asked sarcastically, always one to keep an argument alive.

Ella did know that Pops would've been disappointed in her sister's spending choices, and that is because she had spent much more time with him than Charlotte. They had a bond that was shaped by the many afternoons they spent together while Charlotte was at dance practices. Every day at 3:00 p.m., when Ella got home from her shift at the local ice cream shop, Pops was sitting at the kitchen table with a hand of cards ready to be shuffled and dealt to his granddaughter.

With the news playing in the background at all times, Pops would dole out tidbits of advice, sparked by the top stories being announced by the anchor. Whether the newscaster was recounting a local business closure or was among a crowd of people lined up to purchase the latest technology, the conversations between Pops and Ella undoubtedly always led to him offering up bits of advice that Ella happily applied to her own life throughout the years. Charlotte was closer to their grandmother, since they both shared their love of dance.

"Char, I'm not trying to be a downer, but before you got this money, you were calling me quite regularly asking me to bail you out of a bill you couldn't pay; maintaining minimum payments on your credit cards isn't an ideal situation to begin with." Ella paused, leaning into the silence on the other end of the line. "Char, I'm worried about you."

What Are Charlotte's and Ella's Money Narratives?

I am the youngest of five children. Over the years I've observed how my siblings and I remember childhood stories differently, often putting our own spin on the outcome, polishing, or abbreviating a scene that unfolded in the past with our own personalized perspective.

How can one event translate so differently?

Like Ella and Charlotte, we all have vastly different views that are shaped by our experiences. In this story, each girl gathered pieces of their personal narrative that rolled into their future priorities over time.

$ $ $

There are times in my life when I feel more relatable to Charlotte and times when I identify more with Ella. The result of each girl's story could have spun off in many directions.

What if Charlotte made it big as a professional dancer and ended up building wealth through fame and fortune? What if Ella never had the opportunity to receive the insightful lessons from her grandfather? They individually created their own money narratives based on experiences and knowledge they gained when they were young.

During my career I've witnessed inheritance money passed through many hands, and the outcome is always unique. While these "expected or unexpected windfalls" are never guaranteed, they are a gift, and how the money is used is up to the receiver.

Ella had the good fortune of spending time with her grandfather who shared knowledge that she made good use of and applied to her own life. Ella may also have a natural interest in financial topics whereas Charlotte may not.

Growing up, my two older brothers and I took piano lessons. Ronnie and Jason were musically inclined, and their ability to play the piano expanded to other instruments and careers in the music industry that are still going strong today. I am very proud of my brothers' success and accomplishments, and it always amazed me that they had the gift of music because music didn't make sense to me at all. I love music and going to concerts, but outside of those piano lessons and a short stint on stage as a dancer in their band, the music "gene" was lost on me. As they taught themselves to strum a guitar, I preferred to play pretend "bank," although I rarely had any takers to play it with me. My takeaway from this experience is that we are all born with different interests and natural talents/abilities. I would have to work much harder to get to a basic level with an instrument; Charlotte may feel the same about financial planning topics.

Like all things in life, a problem will remain a problem if it's not addressed with a plan of action. Charlotte may need to experience a financial low before she decides to change things, or worse yet, she may stay in that place her entire life and blame circumstances or bad luck versus bad choices.

Before we can move the needle on financial progress, we need to take ownership of our financial choices and an honest inventory of where we are

> Before we can move the needle on financial progress, we need to take ownership of our financial choices and an honest inventory of where we are and how we got there.

and how we got there. I understand that many dislike money topics and shield themselves in avoidance to the point of discomfort. However, progress can still be made with help to carry the load of emotional money baggage.

I am fortunate that money is a topic I like to talk about. There are many fields of expertise that go right over my head. If I go to the doctor and he tells me there are concerns around various parts of my recent bloodwork, it's as if he's speaking a different language. I do understand actionable steps such as cutting out certain foods and exercising more or taking supplemental vitamins. I do not need to understand the issue to the core depth that he does because I trust him, in the same way my clients trust me to help with steps to improve their financial picture.

You don't need to become an expert on the granular detail of the prescription; you simply need to be a part of the process and want to improve your own overall financial picture versus unnecessary stress and worry that don't really help anyway.

Ella had the good fortune of naturally being interested and receptive to financial advice, and her story shines; Charlotte had a great opportunity for guidance through the process, but she didn't see the value in it at that time in her life. Charlotte is still young, and hopefully she will choose to turn it around for herself and her relationship with her sister. Ella may become resentful if her sister continually asks to borrow money.

Questions to Consider

➤ Do you have any expected windfalls (inheritance dollars) that you are aware of?

➤ Do you and your siblings view money differently?

➤ Do you feel that your views around money are closely aligned to one of your parents or a close family member?

Do

➤ Be aware and question financial beliefs that feel natural but are attached to negative emotions that aren't healthy for you or your family.

➤ Have conversations with your partner, spouse, close friends, and family members about general financial beliefs and any early childhood stories that may support these general thoughts (i.e., money is good, money is bad/evil, money is neutral).

➤ Consider working on any "money narratives" that aren't supporting your goals.

➤ Incorporate any inheritance money into your overall plan *after* you receive it.

Don't

➤ Beat yourself up if you are not where you want to be. Money narratives can change once we start listening to the stories we tell ourselves.

➤ Treat a windfall like it's "different money" or "not your money." Once you receive an inheritance, it is yours and should be treated like your other money.

➤ Count on an inheritance as a "way out" of other poor decisions. Anything can happen, and there are no guarantees.

We all have a choice over our financial decisions and the legacies we want to leave behind. It won't necessarily happen overnight, but to make positive changes, we have to be aware of the financial narratives that might be sabotaging our goals and work to improve them. There is always hope; change doesn't happen overnight, but with small changes over time, you will be amazed at how quickly a rhythm and new habits will form. Most people wait until New Year's to attack new goals, but I think the best time to make changes is when the thoughts around your finances are tugging at you and you know changes are needed. Now is always better than next week or next year.

15

LINKING THE LEGACY

L IKE EVERY NEW YEAR'S EVE SINCE 1985, THE
beach cottage was bustling with activity. On one side
of the living room, Evan, Nick, and James gathered
around a puzzle table, inserting pieces as they chatted about
their past years in business.

James released an exhale as he sat back in his chair and
broke away from the puzzle to take a sip of the beach house
holiday signature cocktail—some concoction made with
eggnog that always had a bright, papery umbrella stuck in a

piece of floating pineapple. He still wasn't sure if he liked it, but it was a tradition for the family.

This was the first time he'd been able to really celebrate a New Year's Eve free of stress in five years. His divorce had left him with a mix of emotions that took a lot of time to sort through. Now, since he'd reached several milestones in his new career as a project manager, he was in a place where he wasn't struggling financially, and he didn't have to stress about his future and, for that matter, his son, Will's, future. His gaze landed on the boy now, one year into college and fully immersed in his studies at a university that was located across the country. He would savor this evening and the days he had with him before he headed back to school.

Will caught his dad watching him and sauntered across the living room, his hand deep in a bowl of caramel popcorn, another traditional staple for the family's holiday gathering. "Hey, Dad, are you getting all teary on me again?" He plopped into a nearby chair.

"Just proud of you, son," James said, making a note of how long Will's limbs were. His legs, stretched out before him, took up nearly all the space in between them.

"Right back at you, Dad." He winked and popped a few more pieces of the caramel corn in his mouth.

"What's everyone talking about?" Rebecca, James's sister, balanced a tray of appetizers. She handed one to her husband, Evan, then set them down on the coffee table and sat in a folding chair that was pulled up for additional seating.

"Oh, I was just telling Dad how proud I was of him. Basically starting his life over from scratch, taking on a new career, buying a condo."

"You've come a long way, brother." Rebecca adjusted the doily on a side table, one of the many decorations she'd added to spice up the space for the party.

"So have you, sister." James passed a genuine smile to his younger sister. He had always been proud of her running her own business, but now even more so since she had really taken it upon herself to make sure she was implementing all the right steps toward success. Financial planning wasn't something that ran in their family, and they both had to figure things out on their own. With the help of their cousin Hudson who had recently been on his own financial journey, the siblings were in a good place. It wasn't easy, but it was well worth it.

Across the room, their cousin Charlotte led some of the third-generation cousins in a ballet routine, and her twin sister, Ella, watched with awe.

"She's still got it, doesn't she?" The voice interrupted Ella's thoughts as she felt her grandmother Sophia's hand settle on her shoulder.

"Yeah, she does." Ella rested a hand on Sophia's, gently rubbing the wedding ring that she still wore. "She must've gotten her perseverance from you." She looked up to see the matriarch of the family smiling down at her.

"My father used to always say, 'Charlotte has her ballet, and Ella has her books.'" Sophia now rested both hands on Ella's shoulders and squeezed them gently.

"Pops was a great man."

"Yes, as was Grandpa Ben." Sophia looked around the room, taking in the warmth of her extended family interacting with one another.

"He'd be pretty impressed with how far you've come too, Grandma."

"He would, wouldn't he?" Sophia stared ahead, thinking about how grateful she was to receive the additional income from renting out the beach house for a portion of the year. She was also grateful for the life insurance that Ben took out on himself to pay off their portion of the mortgage if anything happened to him. She may not be here, gathered around her family on New Year's Eve, if these things were not put in place.

> She was also grateful for the life insurance that Ben took out on himself to pay off their portion of the mortgage if anything happened to him. She may not be here, gathered around her family on New Year's Eve, if these things were not put in place.

Seconds later, the front door of the cottage swung open, filling the room with a blast of cold air. Standing front and center were Abby and her younger cousin, Emma, with her husband, Oliver. Tucked in between the couple was their five-year-old daughter, Eleanor, hidden behind a fluffy winter hat, earmuffs, and thick pink fleece jacket. "The party has arrived!" Abby announced.

"It's about time." Abby's teenage sons looked up from their devices, sauntered across the room, and greeted their mother with a hug. "Dad ran out to get some ice cream for your famous apple pie."

"Well, we're going to need that because we have something big to celebrate," Abby said as she walked effortlessly out of her knee-length wool coat.

A dozen questions flew through the air from the rest of the family members. Oliver and Emma moved into the kitchen area where everyone had gathered, while Eleanor joined the other dancing tots. "We'll let Abby make the announcement, since she is the one who helped execute this plan."

Abby accepted a decorative champagne flute from her cousin Rebecca and tapped the glass gently. "I'm happy to share the exciting news about Oliver and Emma's new addition—"

"Another baby!" Several voices shouted in unison.

"Finally, Eleanor will have a sibling!" Another one joined in.

Abby interrupted the banter and continued. "Actually, nope, it's the addition of their home!"

A hush swam through the crowd, and several sets of eyes peered at her in confusion. Oliver stepped forward, lifting up his own champagne glass. "As you all know, we purchased our first home two years ago, and while we were very grateful for that, we always wanted a bigger home with an office space and another bedroom, in case … we do expand the family—"

"Oh, just say it, Oliver!" Emma's voice punched the air. "We've saved up enough money to add on, and our plans have been approved by our city planning department!"

A ripple of applause, hoots, and hollers filled the air, and then as confusion set in, another question made it through the space. Nick asked, "Wait, but what does this have to do with Abby?"

"Well, since she started investing her time and money into the nonprofit that Oliver works for, she's been teaching us about prioritizing our goals and finances, and we always thought we'd just buy a newer, bigger home, but we really love where we are, and we've already made so many memories there, so we want to stay and expand."

"That's wonderful!" Nick said, pulling his son, Christopher, into his side.

"Hey, Dad, maybe we need an addition so you have a bigger space for your cars," Christopher joked, and the rest of the family erupted into laughter. The conversation about his car hobby had transformed into a friendly one over the years. The more Nick taught Christopher that as long as you have your budget properly prioritized, you shouldn't feel guilt over spending some money on things you love and enjoy. Now that he was approaching the end of college, he was quickly learning that happiness was achieved through a healthy work/life balance.

Interrupting the celebratory hugs was the sound of the doorbell ringing, then the whoosh of the door swinging open again. "Did I miss the party?" Hudson, Abby's younger brother, appeared in the entryway.

"No! In fact, I think we were just getting ready to go over our resolutions," Rebecca piped in. "Everyone, gather in the living room." She led the way and handed everyone a small red box as they sat down.

"Sorry I'm late. I had my annual meeting to assess my financial plan." Hudson pulled Abby into a side hug before he sat on the floor, sandwiched between the Christmas tree and his younger cousin Megan, who was swiping a finger across her new iPad.

"Okay, you all know the rules." Rebecca stood in the center of the circle, holding a red box on display. "You announce your resolution, write it down, then put it in the box and set it under the tree."

Confirmations echoed throughout the circle as everyone went to work removing the small piece of folded paper from the box. "Can I go first this year?" Megan shot her arm up.

"Of course." Rebecca motioned for Megan to kick off the annual game.

"I want to up the money I'm putting in my investment account each month. Since I've opted to go to community college at night while working at the nonprofit during the day, I think it's doable."

"I have no doubts you'll accomplish that," Hudson said, as he knocked into Megan and went to work writing his resolution down.

"Next up ... Abby."

Abby tilted her head to the side, her eyes scanning the ceiling before she spoke. "I'm going to start a fund for family vacations. A place that we can all agree on."

She side-hugged her son and smiled big, knowing deep down inside it was going to be a place where they would make wonderful memories, a place that they would be talking about for years to come. It had been five years since they'd sold their second home, and it was time to start vacationing again.

A half hour later, there was a stack of boxes positioned like a Lego structure beneath the tree, and all but one family member had shared their resolution.

"Grandma Sophia." Rebecca, now seated in the middle of the circle, extended a hand out to the matriarch's position.

Sophia cleared her throat as she rocked back in her late husband Ben's favorite recliner. "I'm going to make sure I take the necessary steps, so I leave a bright legacy behind ... for all of you."

16

THE IMPORTANCE OF HAVING THE RIGHT TEAM

W HEN I STARTED AS AN ADVISOR, I HAD A LOT
to learn. I leaned heavily on others for support
and guidance. One of my early mentors gave
me great advice and told me to identify advisors that I looked
up to and invite them to lunch or approach them at conferences and try to spend a few minutes asking questions, if they
were willing to share.

As a female working in a male-dominated field, there were often very few other women in attendance at industry-related conferences or events. At this previous firm, however, several of our top advisors were women, and this inspired me. When I started attending conferences with the company, I made it my mission to meet as many of our top advisors as I could and ask about best practices and any advice they were willing to share as I was getting started.

I met Cheryl after being in the business for only six months or so. She was a legend at the company and had been there for decades, and I knew who she was, although she didn't know me. I approached her to introduce myself and remember feeling at ease with her warmth and kindness. She could have been dismissive considering the majority of new advisors didn't make it through their first year, but she wasn't. She treated me like an old friend even though she barely knew me. She became a strong role model to me over the years; her generous abundance was contagious, and it was no mystery why she was so successful. It made me happy to see Cheryl and other top female advisors take the stage and be recognized by the company; it motivated and inspired me to continue learning and growing.

Several years later I was invited to join a panel discussion onstage at a company conference. Still young in my career, it was an honor to be invited as one of the chosen few to discuss changes and initiatives that were in process. Elaine, another one of our top female advisors who worked in the same office as Cheryl, would be part of the panel discussion too. I was more than a little nervous about this commitment in front of hundreds of people, but I knew that I couldn't say no. As we prepared to go onstage, I found myself attempting deep breaths and pushing away the fear that was rapidly consuming me.

In just a couple of minutes, the moderator would give us the cue that it was our turn to take our places on stage. Elaine, privy to my unease, approached me and, in a confident and sincere tone, said, "Amy, if you get nervous, look at me and lock eyes with mine and know that we are in this together."

As the session began and I nervously awaited the questions that would be coming soon, I turned my head to face Elaine, and as promised, she was ready for me and set her eyes on mine; in that moment I knew I would be okay. Everything went great, and I am forever grateful for the compassion and kindness in that moment.

In my career and life, I have had many mentors and coaches that have positively impacted my life like Cheryl and Elaine. I don't often get to *publicly* thank them; however, it is very clear to me that I would not be where I am without those who have guided me with their knowledge and served as part of a far greater outcome than I could have done on my own.

Experience and daily exercise are important with any skill set. If a surgeon didn't perform an operation for a few years, it would take time to rebuild skill, routine,

> By surrounding myself with other professionals who are immersed in their area of expertise, my odds of success are enhanced.

and momentum. By surrounding myself with other professionals who are immersed in their area of expertise, my odds of success are enhanced.

When building a financial team, consider adding a financial advisor/planner, CPA, estate-planning attorney, banker, and an insurance agent. Putting the right team in place can prove to be invaluable for long-term success.

Hiring a Financial Advisor

Choosing the right people to add to your financial team is an important decision. On a professional sports team, the coach is highly paid and a critical part of the team even though he or she is not the player. The coach can see things looking in that the players might miss. He can catch habits or movements that the athlete may not realize they are doing. Sometimes, the tiniest little shifts can make a huge difference.

As I mentioned earlier, I have had many mentors and coaches throughout my career; many have never worked as an advisor, but their extensive experience working with other advisors can help me see things I cannot see on my own. I remember one of my coaches telling me that I needed to put some parameters in place within my practice and grow slower and more strategically. In my mind I had it all under control—until I didn't—and his words rang in my ears as I made changes that would have been much easier to address before it was a problem. Similarly, advisors can often identify gaps and potential issues because we are looking in from the outside. As our experience builds, we can see how financial scenarios play out differently and use our professional experience to help others avoid common pitfalls and mistakes.

The word "advisor" is sometimes loosely used in the financial services industry. Similar to the medical and legal field where there are many different subcategories of expertise and specialization, the same is true for advisors.

To help you work through this, I have put together a list of considerations and questions to help.

WHAT TYPE OF ADVISOR DO YOU NEED?

Investment advisors provide personalized advice and help you strategize and choose investments based on your goals, risk tolerance, and time horizon. An investment advisor will manage the investments and review with you for an asset-based fee, which typically is inclusive of trading and rebalancing.

Financial planners provide advice holistically about all aspects of a client's financial life including budgeting, insurance needs, investments, retirement planning, and estate planning. There are financial planners who provide planning services only and others who help implement investment and insurance recommendations in the plan. When hiring a financial planner, a good place to start is cfp.net under "Find a CFP® Professional." You can search by city or zip code, and there will be a brief description about the advisor, minimum requirements, and scope of services they offer. The Certified Financial Planner designation requires extensive additional education and experience on top of basic licensing requirements needed to become an advisor.

Brokers help buy and sell stocks and bonds and are usually paid commissions. Full-service brokerage firms are more expensive and may provide personalized investment advice, while discount brokerage firms have lower fees and commissions but do not help with investment selection. Robo-advisors are brokerage firms with automated investment portfolios based on questions about your risk tolerance and time horizon and lower fees and minimum investment requirements. You will not receive personalized guidance and advice with a Robo-advisor.

Some advisors and brokers are employees of their respective companies and receive a salary plus bonuses based on production requirements. Typically, employee advisors work for large banks. Independent financial advisors are business owners paid on the products and services they implement with clients; they are responsible for their own expenses, overhead, and staff. When you hire an independent financial advisor or financial planner, you are hiring the "person" you choose; when you hire an employee advisor, you hire the company they work for.

Fiduciary Duty versus the Suitability Standard

Investment advisor representatives registered with the US Securities and Exchange Commission (SEC) are required to act as fiduciaries with their clients. Fiduciaries are required to act in their clients' best interest when making recommendations and avoid conflicts of interest. In a nutshell, a fiduciary duty requires an advisor to act in your best interest versus the advisor's bottom line.

Not all advisors are fiduciaries; many are brokers or financial sales representatives held to a "suitability standard," which means that products offered must be "suitable" for your goals, but they are not required to ensure that the products are in the client's best interest or avoid conflicts of interest.

There are designations that require advisors to act as a fiduciary to maintain their designation. For example, Certified Financial Planner professionals are held to a fiduciary standard by the CFP Board of Standards.

Advisory Compensation and Fee Structures

Fee-only: Fee-only advisors may charge flat fees, hourly fees, or a percentage of the assets they manage for you. Financial planning fees are typically fee-only. Asset management fees are based on the value of the account and typically include all trading, rebalancing, and ongoing management.

Registered investment advisors are fee-only and have a fiduciary duty to their clients.

Commission-based: With this structure, advisors earn commissions based on products sold to clients. Examples of commission-based products include the following:

- Mutual funds with up-front "loads" or sales charges.

- Brokers earn commissions through executing individual equity or bond trades.

- Insurance agents earn commissions from selling insurance products.

- Insurance agents are held to the "suitability standard" versus fiduciary duty.

Fee-based: Advisors who are fee-based fall under a combination of both structures and are often referred to as "hybrid" or "dual-registered." A dual-registered advisor is both a registered representative with a broker-dealer (suitability standard) and an investment advisor representative (fiduciary duty), and many also hold an insurance license if they assist clients with implementing insurance product needs.

Resources

There are many certifications in financial services, and the requirements to obtain them can vary quite a bit. To research a specific designation, you can go to the Financial Industry Regulatory Authority (FINRA) website: https://www.finra.org/investors/professional-designations.

Information about financial advisors' experience, licensing, and public disciplinary action (if applicable) is available through FINRA's BrokerCheck and SEC's Investment Adviser Public Disclosure databases.

Questions to Ask a Potential Financial Advisor/Planner

➥ How are you registered (investment advisor representative, broker, insurance agent)?

➥ Will you have a fiduciary duty to me?

➥ What licensing and professional designations do you hold?

➥ What is your investment philosophy? Are there any limitations to the investment options you have access to?

➥ What services do you offer, and do you engage in *comprehensive* financial planning? Do you help implement plan recommendations?

➥ How are you paid for your services? Commission, fee based, or a blend of both?

➥ How many clients do you have, and what type of clients do you typically work with?

➥ How often will we meet or review? Will this be in person, via Zoom, or by phone? Will I be meeting with you or other members of your team?

➥ Do you have a minimum to take on new clients?

➥ If something happens to you, who will manage my accounts? Do you have a contingency plan in place?

Whether you are just starting out or financially savvy, a financial advisor can be a valuable addition to your team to help navigate the ever-changing environment of options and resources.

I recommend interviewing two or three advisors before making a decision. Choose someone you trust and who is willing to spend time explaining things to ensure you are comfortable with the process and decisions you are making. While experience, education, and credentials are important considerations, this is a big decision and a relationship that could last for decades, so make sure that you feel good about it. There are a lot of excellent financial advisors out there, but every potential client isn't a good fit for every advisor; a mutual fit is a win for both the advisor and the client in the long term.

Your financial team serves as an umbrella over your financial picture; as your picture evolves, your team will likely grow too. When you are getting started, you may have a banker and an insurance agent. As the complexity of your plan grows, you build your team with a tax professional, financial planner, investment advisor, and estate-planning attorney to optimize your growth over time.

17

YOUR MONEY NARRATIVE

F
IRST OF ALL, IF YOU ARE READING THIS CHAPTER, I want to thank you for taking the time to read the book. I know that there are a million books about money and finance out there, and I'm grateful that you chose this one. I hope this book can serve as a relatable guide and inspiration to check off a couple of boxes on your "to-do" list.

Since becoming an advisor, my consistent goal has been to simplify the process of financial planning in an industry that uses many complex words and concepts that can be a little intimidating and even overwhelming. Frankly, I simplify as much as I can so that I can understand it too.

I hope this book will spark some great conversations and thoughts around your own money narratives. If you take action on a couple of ideas sparked from the stories in this book, I would consider that a huge success!

As you reflect on your own money narrative, consider some of the following questions:

➤ What is your earliest memory about money? Is it a positive memory? Why?

➤ When you were young, were financial topics openly discussed or not discussed at all? Why?

➤ Is your money style more aligned with one parent versus the other? Why?

➤ Have you ever made a financial decision based on outcomes you witnessed growing up? Was it positive or negative? Why?

➤ Do you fear not having enough money? Why?

➤ How much money would be "too much"? Why?

➤ While reading this book, did any other recollections surface that pertained to money? Why?

➤ Is there a difference in your money style versus your siblings? What about your spouse? Why?

➤ What stories in the book were most relatable? Why?

➤ Were there any stories that reminded you of someone close to you? Why?

➤ Do you enjoy talking about financial topics or avoid them? Why?

➤ What is the best financial decision you have ever made? Why?

➤ What is the worst financial decision you have ever made? Why?

➤ What is your number one financial goal right now? Why?

The goal is to gain awareness and perspective. Awareness so you can start making some connections and perspective so that you can decide if they are helping you reach your goals or if you need to put a few stories on the shelf to make room for new ones.

Why do I ask, "Why?"

I'm glad you asked! I love the word "why"; it has been both a friend and foe to me in life.

For anyone who has children, do you remember when your sweet little babies started speaking? They start with "Dada" and "Mama" and then they move to "no" and "Why?" Babies ask "Why?" out of curiosity; they want to understand the big and daunting world around them. Understanding the "why" increases security and confidence.

As we get older, we form our belief system and often stop questioning things as much as we did at three or four. When I started diving into personal self-development, I found myself asking "Why?" a lot, which can be annoying to others at times.

Why do we forget how to be curious? Being curious can be an incredible resource for resolving issues and escaping a stagnant routine. Curiosity can help you find new ways to get where you want to go. It may be a little uncomfortable, but embracing discomfort is worth it to continue to make strides toward your goals.

Consider questioning some of your own stories and try the *why* exercise (Why do I think this is the only way, the only solution, the absolute truth?). If the answer isn't logical or doesn't make sense, keep asking until it does. You may end up laughing and saying, "That story doesn't make any sense!"

No matter your age or stage, it's never too late. If you are still here, there is still time.

As a reminder, the checklists are available via my website at www.YourMoneyNarrative.com or through the QR code to help with financial preparedness and action steps.

Thank you again for reading this book. I wish you the best of luck with your continued financial planning and discovering your own money narrative!

With gratitude,

AMY COOK

Your Money Narrative
www.YourMoneyNarrative.com

ACKNOWLEDGMENTS

MY CLIENTS—THANK YOU FOR YOUR TRUST, your friendship, and choosing me to be a part of your team; I'm grateful to be a part of each and every one of your lives. It's hard to call it a job when I feel like I'm catching up with old friends. I would not be writing this book or have the incredible business that I do without all of you.

Emma and Abby—I'm so proud of each of you. You have been my inspiration and purpose and the two best decisions of my entire life.

Giancarlo Foti—one of my earliest mentors, my friend, and my love—thank you for your huge heart, adoration, and encouragement.

Mom—I can't imagine choosing to have a fifth kid, but I'm happy you did—thanks for teaching me so many valuable lessons and always being a strong support, friend, and mother.

Kimber O'Shea—KMA! You are an amazing sister and my best friend. I appreciate all of our conversations dissecting so many things; you are the most talented person I know.

Keith, Ronnie, and Jason—I am thankful to share my earliest memories with you, my brothers. You hold a special place in my heart; I love you and am proud of all you have accomplished.

Travis Raisch—I feel blessed to have met you. Your expertise and support have been invaluable over the years.

Joe Borriello—you have an enviable skill set and an even bigger heart. Thank you for all you do.

Financial advocates—you *all* are amazing! Special thanks to Angie Vlach, Gary Campbell, Matt Lazaras, Ron Mendoza, and Ryan Zimmerman; I am grateful for your continued support and so glad we met when we did.

Karl Bobo—I hold our friendship and your infinite wisdom near and dear to my heart. I miss working with you.

Tom Jones—without you, I would not have had the opportunity to work with some of the coolest people out there. Thank you for your wisdom and trust in my capabilities very early in my career.

John Walker—you have the gift of inspiration, and your exceptional leadership over a short time was impactful and encouraging. I'm thankful that we crossed paths at CDC in KC.

Cheryl Marquez—you are an amazing woman on top of your extraordinary success as an advisor; thank you for being such an incredible role model and leader, for your generous heart, and for all the help over the years.

Elaine Manley—thank you for your wisdom and kindness on that stage when I needed it. You are an admirable advisor, and I'm happy I had the opportunity to observe your success and learn from you.

John Cordeiro—you made it all look so easy! I have always looked up to you and admire your approach to advising and running your practice. I appreciate the time you spent helping me over the years.

Brian Fields—thank you for the years of mentorship, picking up the phone when I needed a friend, and always being a fan. I will never forget the support from you and other leaders who helped me to grow along the way.

BRN 1—you guys are the best! It has been fun collaborating with you over the past decade. I appreciate your friendship and support over the years. To the early trendsetters—Ray, Roger, Lynnel, Chris (Nicole, Maureen)—will we still be meeting in twenty years?

Cheryl Angeles—it has been fun working with you over the years; I learned so much about the nonprofit world in our time together. I hope you take some amazing trips in retirement and enjoy your well-deserved downtime.

Will Bohne—your planning expertise has been invaluable to the team, and we appreciate all that you do.

Ben Mossman—thank you for going above and beyond to help over the years; I am thankful for your friendship, support, and Excel mastery skillset. I wish you and Tate much success with What's Next.

Chief Manheimer—I feel blessed that I got to spend time with you over the years. Thank you for all that you did to protect our community and for being an amazing and strong role model to me and others.

David Pelzner—you are a true professional and a valuable resource; thank you for being part of my "financial team" and for helping so many others.

Michael Berube—I will always appreciate you working with me on such a short timeline to create a beautiful space. Many thanks to you and Chonita for all you do to help small businesses flourish.

Tayo Wilson-Anumudu—thank you for taking such good care of the girls when they were little; I never had to worry when you were in charge. It has been fun to see your success and growth in your life and career.

Shannon Dwyer—you have a remarkable gift of perception and understanding. I am so glad I met you and grateful for your friendship and insight. Thank you for everything.

Amy Rush—your support, guidance, and willingness to go above and beyond to help over the years helped me tremendously; you are the best in your field.

Julie Sagatelian—thank you for taking me "under your wing" in Kansas City at that first conference many years ago; it meant the world to me!

Janelle Bergstrom—thank you for our work together in the early years; you are an incredible resource, and your help was invaluable.

Richard Davey—you are a great advisor, Richard. It was a pleasure working with you and getting to know you in the early years.

Spenser Garrison—it was great working with you and collaborating; I appreciate your friendship through the years.

Shawn Mihal—thank you for bringing hope and transparency during times of uncertainty; your principles and ethics are appreciated.

Jason Gryder—ah, the good old days! I value our time working together and collaborating years ago and all the fun we had.

Ryan Wells—I'm happy our paths crossed; your optimism and endless energy are contagious. The world of business is fortunate to have you.

Tammy Ellegard-Hewes—your support and friendship throughout the years have been invaluable. I'm thankful for the circumstances that brought us together.

Kimberly Wright—you have the gift of encouragement, and your energy is contagious; I am thankful for our friendship.

PL&L—Betty Jo Waxman and Lindon Crowe—you both have helped me so much over the years with your insight and commitment to helping others grow into extraordinary people.

Kate Anslinger—I'm so happy we met. This book would not have happened without your talent and flair.

David Meerman Scott—your mentorship and guidance have been a gift; thank you for your leadership and willingness to shepherd me in a positive direction.

The book project team—A special thanks to each of you who worked so hard to make this book happen. To the talented group at Advantage Forbes Books, Jacob and Lauren in editorial, Wesley in design, and Corrin and Harper in book promotions, for your guidance. To Trivuj at 99 Designs, for your design work on the cover and other images, and to Emma for the additional input and design flair in creating the website design and a number of images.

Some of the amazing inspirational thinkers who inspire me—Dave Ramsey, Tony Robbins, Brené Brown, Jean Chatzky, Thomas Stanley, Carl Richards, David Mullen, David Bach, and Adam Grant.

ABOUT THE AUTHOR

Amy R. Cook is a collector of many things, including knowledge. She spends her time immersed in her financial planning practice and likes to travel and work on hobby projects in her free time. She is currently building a dollhouse and working on a series of children's books about collections (Lessons in Collections), spurred by her love of vintage and antique things that started when she was a child and spent weekends exploring antique stores with her parents.

Her arrival in the financial industry was a serendipitous chain of events that started with her own money narrative and transformed into a success story. While working in the mortgage business at the start of her career, she was exposed to many financial dilemmas and noticed a reactive approach to financial decision-making.

She began to see that money was not something that needed to be reclaimed and put back together. Proactively, it was something that could be controlled and tackled with a solid plan and a grip on the narrative that runs through our minds. Since then, she has aimed to simplify the process of financial decisions and planning to help her clients reach their goals.

When she started her career as a financial advisor in 2009, her drive to overcome her own money narrative bolstered her passion to help clients dissect their goals and lay down a track that is free from unrealistic expectations yet layered in attainable goals that help take them from their starting point to beyond retirement.

Amy credits her unwavering interest in financial planning to lessons she has learned in her own life and a commitment to helping others do the same. Amy is a CFP® and has a master's degree in personal financial planning. She utilizes her education and experience to help clients across all industries and in all stages of life. Just like our individual circumstances, she believes financial planning is dynamic and ever changing, and preparation is key.

Amy lives and works in San Mateo, California, serving clients throughout the country from her local office.

WWW.YOURMONEYNARRATIVE.COM